Talking together...

... about sex and relationships

A practical resource for schools and parents working with young people with learning disabilities

by Lesley Kerr-Edwards and Lorna Scott

fpa

putting sexual health on
the agenda

Acknowledgements

fpa and the authors would like to thank:

The parents, staff and headteachers of:
Avalon School, Street, Somerset
Fiveways School, Yeovil, Somerset
Furzedown School, Winslow, Bucks
Park School, Aylesbury, Bucks
for their involvement in the consultation phase of the book.

Rebecca Johns, whose story work for Image in Action informed some of the ideas in the book.

Sarah Andrews, **fpa**
Toni Belfield, **fpa**
Susan Carini
Nonie Covill
John Drury, Barnardo's
Sarah Duigan, Image in Action
Claire Fanstone, **fpa**
Jane Fraser
Georgie McCormick, **fpa**
Juliana Slobodian, Image in Action
Kim and Cheryl Wyatt
for their helpful comments on the text.

fpa gratefully acknowledges funding from the Diana, Princess of Wales Memorial Fund, the Abbey National Charitable Trust and the Gatsby Charitable Foundation for the production of this resource.

Talking together... about sex and relationships
is published by **fpa**
50 Featherstone Street
London EC1Y 8QU
Tel: 020 7608 5240
Fax: 0845 123 2349
www.fpa.org.uk

© **fpa** 2007

British Library Cataloguing in Publication Data
A catalogue record of this book is available from the British Library.

ISBN: 1 905506 12 0

Illustrations by Nic Watts © Nic Watts
Designed and typeset by Meg Palmer, Third Column
Printed by Newnorth Print Ltd

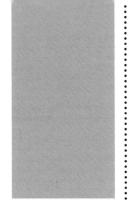

Contents

Introduction

For all of us, growing up is hard to do. It's particularly hard for young people with learning disabilities. Among many other things it means coping with a lot of confusing feelings, sorting out all sorts of relationships – and learning about sex.

This book has been written to support parents and schools as they help older adolescents to understand what is happening to them and to grow up safely and with confidence. It is a companion volume to *Talking together … about growing up*[1] which was written for parents of young people with learning disabilities around the age of puberty. This book takes us to the next stage, as young people are becoming more independent, increasing their range of relationships, thinking about leaving school, and developing their sexuality. A third volume, *Talking together … about contraception*[2], is available to support young people with learning disabilities who wish to access contraception.

Talking together … about sex and relationships also aims to encourage partnership between schools and parents as they both work to make the transition into adulthood easier and more comprehensible to their young people with learning disabilities. Learning is made faster and more consistent when home and school work together.

Adolescence is a period of change, and our adolescent teenagers can be very trying at times. It's natural if they want to shut themselves in their bedroom, lock the bathroom door, choose their own clothes and friends. They need to learn to be independent as they grow older. This can be a worrying time for parents and carers who have to tread the delicate line between allowing their children more freedom while trying to reduce the risks.

Their job isn't helped by some of the attitudes in wider society. Although much continues to change, there are still people who believe that sex is not for disabled people, that people with learning disabilities remain somehow childlike, that they do not (or should not) have sexual feelings.

We know that physical sexual development follows much the same pattern in us all, whatever our abilities. For people with learning disabilities, sexual feelings and behaviours may happen rather later than the norm. They may develop crushes in later adolescence and mature sexual feelings may not appear until they are fully adult – but they do happen. We are aware that a satisfying close relationship can enhance the confidence and self-esteem of people with learning disabilities. It's also worth remembering that the years between 16–19 are a time when many young people are exploring their sexuality.

---

1 Scott L and Kerr-Edwards L. *Talking together … about growing up. A workbook for parents of children with learning disabilities*. **fpa** 1999.
2 Scott L and Kerr-Edwards L. *Talking together … about contraception*. **fpa** 2005.

All family backgrounds are different. We will want to bring up our children to share our values, our beliefs, our culture, including our views on sexual behaviour; and we will want schools to respect them too. But whatever their background, all young people will go through similar stages and will look for support from the most significant adults in their lives – their parents.

> **NOTE:** *We have used the term 'parents' in this book to denote all those who undertake long term care of young people with disabilities, whether in domestic or residential situations.*

Who the book is for

Although the storyline focuses on Tom and Debbie at a particular period in their lives, when they are leaving school to go to college, the issues that are explored are relevant to a younger age group too. Adolescence brings all sorts of changes, which start earlier than school leaving age. Sexual awareness and the desire for greater independence, for instance, develop much earlier.

This means that the material in this book is suitable for use with young people from about age 13; those who have reached puberty, are beginning to show an interest in sex and need to understand about sexuality. It is appropriate for a wide range of students across the learning disability spectrum. Those with mild learning disabilities may enjoy reading the stories for themselves, while most of the activities have been used with students with moderate disabilities and more able students with severe learning disabilities. Teachers will be able to adapt them for their own students.

In the first instance, the book is aimed at teachers in schools and colleges for use in the classroom, but there are home/school sections in each chapter which can be copied and sent home for parents and carers, to use with their adolescent children, to support what is being taught in school. Parents may welcome copies of some of the other materials – maybe the picture stories.

Much of the material in chapters one and two on growing up and keeping safe will be welcomed by parents, who often ask for help with these areas. More specific material on sexuality in later chapters is initially intended for use by schools and colleges which can then ask parents to share and support their work. The whole book can usefully be read and used by parents if they so wish.

What's in the book?

Talking together … about sex and relationships follows on from *Talking together … about growing up*, which dealt with aspects of growing up and puberty. It would make sense to cover the areas in the first book before embarking on this book. Chapters in *Talking together … about growing up* included work on these topics: body parts, public and private, keeping safe, feelings, growing up, menstruation and masturbation. *Talking together … about contraception* can be used for more in-depth discussion of the different methods of contraception, and where young people can access them. It is made up of Book One, for people working with or supporting young people with learning disabilities, and Book Two, for young people with learning disabilities.

There are six chapters in *Talking together … about sex and relationships*:

1   **Preparing for adulthood** – preparing for leaving school and going to college.

2   **Learning to keep safe** – changing situations that can arise with greater independence.

3   **Relationships** – a growing circle of different types of relationships.

4   **All about sex** – understanding sexuality and sexual behaviour.

5   **Sexual choices and sexual health**.

6   **What does the future hold?** – possibilities in adulthood.

Each of the six chapters contains these elements:

—   An introduction to the content of the chapter, and some of the issues for home and school.

—   A storyline with pictures.

—   Activities for use at school or home, or both.

—   Notes with more information on the subject.

—   Suggestions for things to do at home.

A note on classroom methods

Much of the material in this book deals with matters of sexuality and sexual behaviour. It's important therefore that care and sensitivity are used in the classroom so that respect, confidentiality and security are maintained for all concerned, both students and teachers. We use role play and other powerful techniques that have been successfully developed by Image in Action, intended to distance material from the personal and from the individuals in the group. We talk of 'them' rather than 'us', of 'her' rather than 'me'. For more information on distancing techniques, role play and storytelling, and the use of these methods in the classroom, refer to *Let's Do It*, published by Image in Action.[3]

Partnership with parents/carers

The material in this book has been designed to help schools work closely with parents for the benefit of young people, with sections that contain activities particularly suitable for use at home.

---

3   Johns R et al. *Let's Do It: creative activities in sex education for young people with learning disabilities*. Image in Action 1997.

Parents are the first educators of their children, and young people say they want their parents to talk to them about sex; but every survey in the last 20 years has shown that parents want schools to help them to teach their children about sex. For young people with learning disabilities, a strong partnership provides a consistent message from home and school and means that material which has been taught at school can be practised in the reality of the home situation.

Many parents struggle to help their learning disabled children as they grow into adults, and welcome all the support they can find. They want their children to grow into safe, happy adulthood, with stable and satisfying relationships; and they turn to schools to carry out, with them, this challenging task.

Some things can be particularly problematic for parents, like the language to use for body parts and functions. Is it OK to continue to use the 'family' words or should we insist on the 'proper' words as our children grow older? Are these words we are happy using ourselves? How happy do we feel with explicit and detailed illustrations of sexual activities? How closely would we like schools to stick to our particular religious and cultural beliefs and practices?

These issues, and others, will have to be discussed and negotiated by schools in their dealings with parents. Here are some strategies which are examples of good practice in developing effective partnerships with parents and carers.

Informing parents/carers

Every school should have a policy for Sex and Relationships Education (SRE). A brief summary can be sent to every home. Information about the SRE programme can be included in the school newsletter, telling parents what their child will be learning each term. Handouts can be sent with information about 'What we're doing this term', or 'Suggestions for things to do at home'.

Consulting parents/carers

Policies need regular updating. This can be an opportunity to engage parents in discussion about the SRE programme. They can be invited to a consultation meeting, or asked to complete a checklist of their children's needs.

Running a parents' meeting on SRE

This can be an evening meeting for all parents or a smaller event for parents of a particular age group. Some schools find a coffee morning works well. The aim of such meetings is to give information about what the school is doing, and to find out from parents what they think their children need to learn. An outline programme for such a meeting is given opposite, including ideas for activities that will help parents to explain their views.

The checklist on the following page can be used as part of the meeting, or sent home for parents to complete.

A structure for a consultation meeting with parents and carers about the school policy and programme

This programme will take about an hour

Aims

- to inform parents and carers of the proposed policy and programme of sex and relationships education
- to find out what parents and carers see as the sex and relationships education needs of their children
- to invite their views on issues of concern about the sexual development of their children.

Introduction

- Explain the purpose of the meeting, and the proposed policy development envisaged (for example, working party etc).
- Outline ground rules for the session (for example: not breaking confidentiality of their own children; and 'what's said in this room stays in this room' etc).

Who's here?

- Adapt a name game used with students, for example in a circle:

   'I'm ——— and I'm ——— 's parent/carer'

Consultation about the sex and relationships education programme

Step 1
Each person completes the checklist (see p xi), then compares what they have written with a partner. This is followed by some general comments: it is useful to focus on those statements on which pairs have disagreed.

Step 2
In small groups (no more than four per group); each group with a large sheet of paper.

> *Instruction:* Write down everything you think your children should learn about their bodies, their physical development and their sexual development before they leave school. (It may be helpful if a member of staff is part of each group.) Then all papers are displayed and compared.

> *Next:* Each group decides the four most important items from the lists; and each group's choices are marked on sheets displayed. This will give information which the working party can use in their planning.

Step 3

In the same or different small groups:

What are the main concerns of parents and carers about the sexual development of their sons and daughters?

These are written up and displayed, clarified and discussed.

Step 4

In the same or different small groups:

Are there particular things you would like the school to take into account when teaching sex and relationships education to your children?

These are written up and displayed, clarified and discussed.

The feedback from Steps 3 and 4 can be used to inform future planning and policy.

Ending

A round: 'I've found this meeting helpful because ….'

What does your child need to learn about sex?

A checklist for parents and carers

How old is your child? _____

Is your child a girl or a boy? _____

Place a tick beside anything that applies to your child. We will use this information to help us plan the sex and relationships education programme for children in this school.

- [ ] personal hygiene
- [ ] making choices
- [ ] appropriate behaviour eg how to greet people
- [ ] understanding the difference between public and private
- [ ] learning to say 'no'
- [ ] rejecting unwanted approaches
- [ ] recognising and naming feelings
- [ ] names of body parts
- [ ] differences between male and female bodies
- [ ] learning about periods and sanitary pads
- [ ] learning about wet dreams
- [ ] learning about masturbation
- [ ] how the body works (sexually)
- [ ] learning about relationships
- [ ] sexual activity
- [ ] contraception
- [ ] sexually transmitted infections
- [ ] dealing with prejudice

Using this book with parents

While most of the material in this book is suitable for use with a group of students in a teaching situation, much of it is intended either specifically for parents to use, or written so that it can be shared with them to support and reinforce what is being taught.

Storylines about Tom and Debbie, their friends and families, form the core of the book, and provide the context for discussing situations adolescents may find themselves in, and raising issues about sexuality and sexual behaviour. They are followed by activities which develop the theme of each chapter. Some chapters have a section on further information, where relevant, and each ends with suggestions for *Supporting work to do at home*. These may include using the same, or adapted, classroom activities as well as ideas specific to home.

It is up to the school to decide what might be appropriate to send home at any given stage in the programme. We would certainly recommend that parents be consulted, at a meeting or otherwise, before the programme is planned. Ways the school intends to work with parents can be explained, together with the purpose of sending material home; and the benefits of partnership can be extolled.

At the very least, the *Supporting work* pages can be sent home. It may be judged that parents would be able to go through the stories again, and explain to their children their own religious or cultural views on the situations described. Some parents may welcome the further information provided. All this material is free to copy for parents' use.

CHAPTER 1

Preparing for adulthood

This chapter introduces the two main characters in our story: Tom and Debbie. Debbie is already at college and Tom is preparing to leave school and go to college. This is a big change in the lives of young people, and leaving school can be a marker for increasing independence and changing relationships.

The chapter focuses on the changes that are involved in making the move from school to college; with growing independence come more choices, and more responsibility for their own appearance and behaviour.

This time can be a particularly anxious one for parents and carers, who have to watch their adolescents leave the security of school and home to enter a new world with new people, new expectations and new risks. There are some suggestions about ways in which families can help to prepare their adolescents for these new experiences.

Although the storyline follows the lives of two older students, these changes do not begin when young people leave school; and the material in this chapter, and indeed in the rest of the book, will be appropriate for students from about age 13, when moves towards independence, and sexual feelings, become more apparent.

The material in this chapter discusses these areas:

> ⮕ **the differences between adolescence and adulthood**
>
> ⮕ **supporting young people in becoming more independent**
>
> ⮕ **negotiating a wider range of choices**
>
> ⮕ **keeping healthy: food, personal hygiene.**

ACTIVITY 1

Introducing Tom and Debbie

These picture stories introduce our two characters and give a few pointers about their lives. Both are aged 18+ and are at the post school stage.

How to do it

➲ Introduce Tom and Debbie by reading the picture stories on pp 3–4.

➲ Make a list of changes suggested by the class between life as a child at school and life as a student at college.

➲ Show the Before and After drawings. Start with the drawing of Tom as a child (pic 5, p 5)

➲ Ask the class to describe what his life might be like: at home, at school, his hobbies, his clothes etc. Repeat this with the drawing of Debbie as a child.

➲ Show the drawings of Tom and Debbie at 18, one at a time. Ask the class to say what might be different about their lives now: friends, travel, music, clothes etc.

What if?

Your students' family circumstances are different from those in the stories?

➲ Emphasise that the stories are about two imaginary people. Make it clear that everyone's families are different. If necessary, change the status of the adults in the pictures: a carer or an aunt or uncle instead of Mum, for instance.

Many of your students are unlikely to go to college?

➲ Make the discussion about the Before and After drawings more appropriate to your group. Reiterate that the Tom and Debbie stories are not about real people. Explain that some people go to college, while others do different things.

Other things you can do

➲ Use this opportunity to clarify what people can do legally once they are 18: vote, drink in a pub etc.

Tom at the football match

This is Tom. He is 18. He left school in the summer and is looking forward to starting college though he is quite shy. He plans to do a course about computers. He enjoys playing football with his friends and goes with his brother Mike to watch their local team.

Tom and Mum shopping

Tom and his mum go shopping for the things Tom will need at college. Tom likes the black bag but Mum is worried someone may try to steal it from him. She hopes he will be able to stand up for himself at college. Tom tells her to relax – he'll be fine.

Debbie at the computer

3

This is Debbie. She is 18 and has been at college for a year to help her improve her reading, writing and maths. She is friendly and chatty and really likes being at college. She is very keen on computers and plans to do a new course at college this year. She hopes it will help her get a job. She loves drawing and her sister Tracey helps her learn how to do great graphics on the computer.

Debbie and Mum at the bus stop

4

Up till now, Debbie's mum has taken her to college every day by car. But Debbie is planning to catch the bus this year. Her mum is worried that Debbie will get lost or forget the bus number. Debbie says she will go with her friend Karen so they remind each other.

Tom aged seven playing with toys

Tom aged 18 in the pub watching a football match on TV

Debbie aged seven playing with toys

Debbie aged 18 shopping with a friend

ACTIVITY 2

Character cut outs

These A4 drawings of Tom and Debbie can be used in a number of ways, showing them in different situations to illustrate work on hygiene, or diet, or appropriate behaviour.

Some examples:

❷ Choosing healthy food

Match the clothed drawing to a picture of a supermarket; or match to food in the college canteen. What do they choose?

Discuss what food Tom or Debbie might buy: sweets or apples; or burger and chips. Do Tom and Debbie know about healthy eating?

❷ Keeping fit

Match the clothed drawing to a picture of watching TV, or of a swimming pool. Which is the healthy activity?

❷ Keeping clean

Match the underwear drawing to a bathroom picture. Appropriate items a person would use in the bathroom can be added, either real objects or pictures: eg deodorant, soap, razor.

❷ Privacy

Match the underwear drawing to a picture of a supermarket, a bedroom, a bathroom. Which are the appropriate private places for someone in their underwear?

Other things you can do

❷ Make links with other areas of the PSHE curriculum, like healthy eating, hygiene, keeping fit.

❷ More work on privacy can be found in *Talking together … about growing up*; about privacy at home, at school, in public places.

9

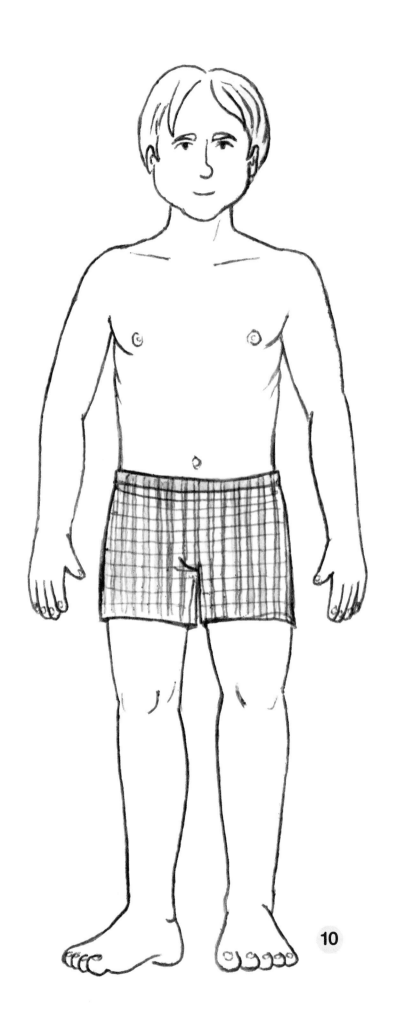

10

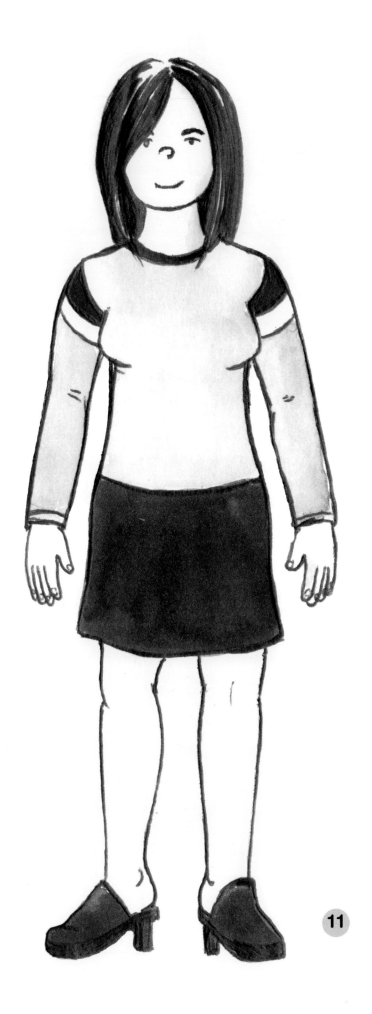

11

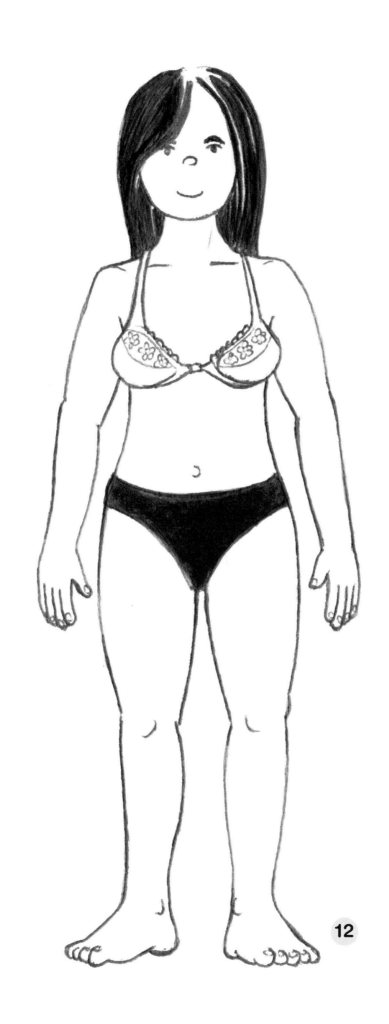

12

Supporting work to do at home

At school your child has been thinking about the changes that take place as we grow from children into adults. This can be a difficult time for parents as our children want and need to become more independent. It might be a good idea to get some support, maybe at school, so that we can talk about this with others who are going through similar times. One of the essential things we have to do as parents is to help to prepare our young people for some of the new situations they face. Here are some suggestions.

❷ Going shopping

Some new toiletries can often indicate a change in status. This may be a good time to buy personal hygiene items and encourage their use. Make sure the choices are made by your son or daughter.

❷ Ways of letting go

Are there other choices to be made? Perhaps your child's bedroom can be turned into a bedsitting room. Local unaccompanied journeys might be encouraged, perhaps to a nearby relative or friend. Are there some evening activities where young people can gather safely without families?

❷ Creating social opportunities

Leaving school or going to college usually means meeting new people, often in larger numbers. It helps if young people have had opportunities beforehand to be part of larger gatherings, with encouragement to practise appropriate social behaviour. Wider family occasions can be useful, as can introducing new situations and activities (below).

❷ Practising routes to college

We can help by sorting out bus timetables and making the journey a few times with the young person. Is there a friend living locally who makes the same journey? What about suggesting they travel together?

❷ Doing new things

Dealing with change can be hard so try to introduce your growing teenager to new activities and situations and take a step back to see how they deal with it. For example:

— Go to a different swimming pool at the weekend – how do they work out where to pay, where to get changed, how the lockers work? Shop in a different place so that they have to find out where the clothes shops are.

— Introduce them to new people and let them speak for themselves, even if they get tongue tied or embarrassed. Later you can practise with them how to greet people so they can try again next time.

— If they are able, let them go on a familiar journey themselves with clear instructions about when to get back.

Before and after

1. Tom and Debbie

Using the relevant drawing of Tom or Debbie on pp 5–6, discuss with your son or daughter what Tom or Debbie might have been like when they were aged around seven (the first drawing).

Then talk about what might have changed, using the second drawing.

For instance:

— **Debbie aged 7:** she goes to school, her mum helps her bath, she never goes anywhere on her own. She has bed times and needs lots of sleep. She eats what her parents make for her. She wears clothes her parents choose. She plays with her toys.

— **Debbie aged 18:** she is grown up. She doesn't play with toys but likes CDs, magazines, computers. She keeps herself clean and is aware of hygiene. She goes out on her own to college or to the park with friends. She buys her own clothes. She decides on her own bed times and can stay up till when she likes though she knows she needs to get plenty of sleep. She does some cooking herself and tries to eat healthy options. She can drink in a pub, she can vote.

Using Tom and Debbie as the starting point talk with your son/daughter about how they have changed/will change as they grow older. Work out together what you can do to encourage this eg allow them to buy their own clothes, learn how to cook simple meals etc.

2. Your child

Find a series of photos of your child as they grow up. Notice the changes.

Find a series of pictures of an adult family member, perhaps yourself, growing up from child to adult. See if your child can point to you at the same age as her/him. See if they can discuss the changes that happened to you as you grew up and use these to discuss changes that may happen to them.

Family collage

Collect photographs of immediate and wider family members over time, showing how people have changed. Include photographs of your son or daughter since babyhood. Can your son or daughter identify themselves and other people at different ages? Talk about how people, and your child, have changed over time. The collage can fill a scrap book.

Future squares

Thinking about the future

Soon your child will become an adult, reaching the age of 18, with all the possibilities and challenges that can bring. Although we often find it difficult to imagine our children as adults, we can help to prepare them for the changes to come.

By filling in this chart with your child or with other people in your family, you may be able to gain some ideas about how things may change in the future and what to be ready for.

- Use the future squares sheet on p 16 or draw one yourself with four sections.

- In section 1 write, draw or use photos or pictures to show what your child is like now.

- Do the same for section 2 showing them in two years' time, section 3 in five years' time and section 4 in 10 years' time.

Other things you can do

- Ask yourself or discuss with someone else in the family, what are the positive things in each square and what are the problems.

- Think about what support you and your child may need at each stage. Find out where you can get this support by asking your child's school, social worker, learning disability services, or specialist self-help groups.

Making the change

There are many things that influence us all as we grow up from children to adults. By thinking about them for our child we can begin to adjust to how life may change for them and for us as they get older.

➔ Use the *Making the change* sheet on p 17 or draw your own.

➔ Put a photo of your child in the centre of the flags.

➔ Fill in the flags with ideas about how your child is influenced by their family, social life, money, school etc.

➔ Then use the sheet again, with an adult figure in the centre, and think about the influences on your son or daughter as an adult.

Compare the two sheets.

Other things you can do

➔ If there are definite changes from one set of influences to another, think how these can come about and what else you may need to find out about. For instance, if home changes from living with family to living independently, how might this happen? What support would your son or daughter need?

Fresh wardrobe

Young people are very fashion conscious especially when they are growing up. This can be a time to have a good look at your child's clothes, together with your son or daughter. Some will no longer fit, while others may now be too childish in style. Remember underwear is important too in helping him/her feel they are growing up, so those Action Man underpants will have to go!

➔ Discuss the possibility of buying two new things that will be for a young adult. Agree what they are before you go out: perhaps a tee shirt and trousers – and how much you are willing to pay!

➔ Make a shopping trip together and help your son or daughter to make the choice. Try to steer them towards clothes for the young adult. It may be helpful to take another teenager along, or an older sibling, who can advise on current teenage style.

Future squares

Now	In two years time
In five years time	In ten years time

Making the change

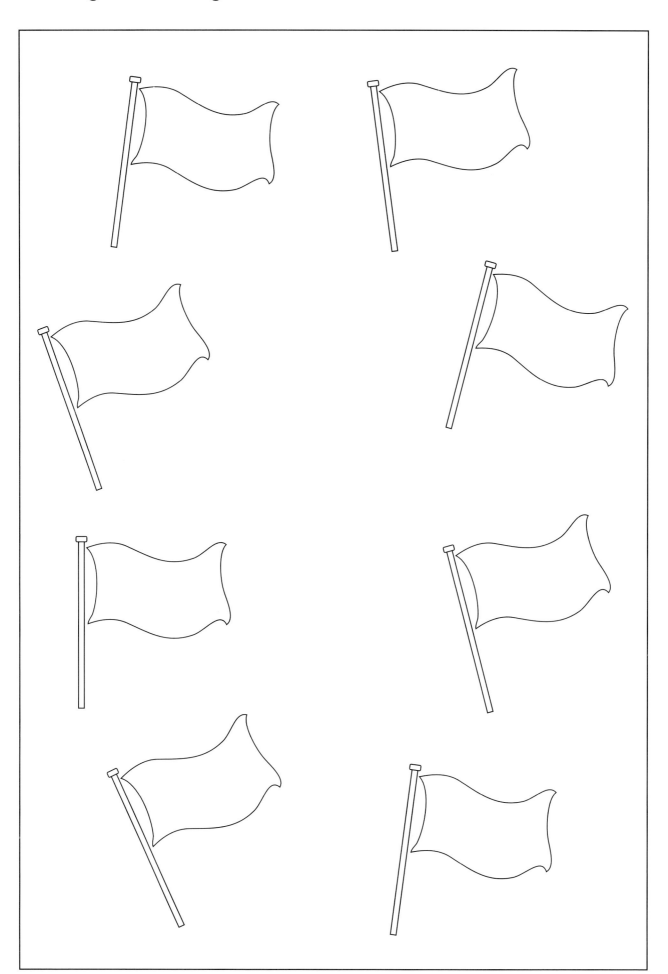

2 Learning to keep safe

Greater independence can place our young people in new situations which they have to learn to interpret and cope with. Sometimes these situations appear relatively harmless; at other times there may be sexual overtones. Knowing how to respond appropriately can be key to success in some awkward spots, and assertion skills are central to this. The activities in this chapter will give practice of using assertion skills in various situations, including those that require a clear understanding of privacy in relation to one's own body.

A big issue for school and home is weighing protection against potential risks. Some risk has to be allowed for any of us to learn, but we are of course concerned that our young people come to no harm. Bullying can be a problem for children in schools of all types, and it will be particularly important that we teach our students strategies for avoiding and dealing with this.

Preparation for making more choices has already been discussed in chapter one: choices about clothes, food, friends, social activities. But families in particular have to manage adolescents who may make what are seen as inappropriate choices: eg 'I want to have my nose pierced' – choices which could lead to difficult situations. Young people with learning disabilities have especial difficulty in understanding other people's feelings and motives, so will need plenty of teaching and reinforcement about potential impressions and responses. The story situations offer opportunities for role playing a range of assertive responses.

The material in this chapter discusses these areas:

> ⬤ **avoiding risky situations: anticipating the risks**
>
> ⬤ **understanding and practising assertion skills.**

What else can they do?

These pairs of pictures show alternative scenarios that provide opportunities to discuss how young people can reduce risks by taking some simple precautions.

› Show the first picture (p 21 or 22) and ask for suggestions from students about what Tom (or Debbie) could have done to avoid the situation arising.

› Show the second picture and clarify the different possible scenarios. Students will enjoy role playing them, and some of their own suggestions too.

› Repeat with the second pair of pictures.

› Assertion work can take place before or after using the story or even better, both. It's a good idea to make sure students know and can use *The rules for saying no*, which were included in *Talking together… about growing up*.

The rules for saying no

› **Stand straight and make definite eye contact.**

› **Say no loudly and clearly.**

› **Don't smile or laugh – be clear that saying no is serious.**

› **Use a firm pushing away hand gesture to reinforce the words.**

Other things you can do

› Discuss particular local 'hot spots' for young people at your school, and any local issues about personal safety.

NOTE: for more information about using role play effectively and safely, see *Let's Do It*, Image in Action 1997.

Tom has taken the short cut to his next class round the back of the building. He notices three boys hanging around there but he keeps going. As he comes past they stop him. They demand that he gives them his mobile phone which they can see in his pocket. Tom doesn't know what to say. He is frightened. They snatch the phone and run away. Tom is upset.

What else could Tom do?

Tom and a friend walking confidently away from the alley where the boys are lurking. The mobile phone is hidden.

- Tom can walk with a friend.
- Tom can make sure his phone is out of sight in a zipped inside pocket.
- Tom can avoid walking through places he doesn't know well and which could be unsafe.
- Tom can walk away quickly if he sees people he doesn't like coming up to him.
- Tom can learn about how people look and move so he knows if someone is likely to be friendly or aggressive.
- Tom can say 'No, go away! I don't know you. It's my phone.' He can shout 'Help! they are stealing my phone.'
- Tom can tell an adult he trusts about the problem.

Debbie has finished college for the day. She is waiting at the bus stop in the rain. A car drives up and stops. A man leans out and says 'Hello there, you look soaking wet. Can I give you a lift home? You remember me don't you? I work in the shop at the bottom of your road. I could drop you off'. Debbie says 'Thanks' and gets in the car. The driver then drives off but not in the direction of Debbie's house. She can't get out of the car. She is frightened and upset.

What else can Debbie do?

Debbie and Karen are waiting for their usual bus. They are dry under their umbrella. When someone offers them a lift they firmly say no. They both support each other.

> Debbie will never get into a car with someone she doesn't know.

> Debbie does not change her travel plans. Her mum is expecting her home on this bus.

> Debbie can refuse to speak to the driver or say 'Go away, I don't know you' in a loud voice.

> Debbie can travel with her friend Karen so they can look after each other.

> Debbie can carry a coat or umbrella so she is prepared for bad weather.

ACTIVITY 2 Is it a problem?

Finding ways to avoid difficult situations is often the best approach. Use these pictures to help students recognise some potential problems.

- Using one picture at a time ask if students notice anything that might cause a problem. What is happening that could mean someone could be putting themselves into a difficult position?

  Picture 5: Underwear showing

  Picture 6: Dressed to draw attention to sexual body parts

  Picture 7: Flies undone

- Once they have understood the problem, ask them what could be done differently.

- Some other scenes to discuss:

  — **Mobile sticking out of Tom's pocket.**

  — **Debbie at the bus stop, with her bag open and her purse sticking out.**

  — **Choosing which way to walk home: down a lighted street or the short cut through an alley with no lights.**

- Use role play to explore these situations.

- Other situations can be suggested by students.

Discussion

- — **Appropriate dress: do views of young people and adults differ? If so, why?**

  — **Does choice of clothes depend on the situation and context?**

  — **Does clothing draw attention to physical development?**

Is it a problem?

5

6

7

No, that's private

It's worth reinforcing the message of this activity, which appeared in a slightly different form in *Talking together… about growing up*, with our older teenagers, who can be confused and distressed by inappropriate touching. Knowing when and how to say No is another aspect of assertion.

This is a game similar to the well known 'Simon says … '. Make sure students know the names of body parts before you use this game.

How to do it

➤ Standing in a circle, the teacher asks everyone to touch a part of their body: 'In this group, is it OK to touch … ?' using a public body part to begin. If it is OK, everyone touches that part of their body.

➤ The teacher repeats this with different non-private body parts very quickly.

➤ A member of staff is asked: 'Can you touch your ………… (name a private part of the body)?' The member of staff models the response 'NO THAT'S PRIVATE' assertively and acting cross.

➤ The students practise the refrain. It creates a strong and positive group atmosphere if the entire group says the phrase at the same time. Encourage the students to use a strong voice and hand gesture and to make their expression look assertive.

➤ The game is repeated using mainly non-private parts of the body, calling out a private body part every now and then as if to catch the group out.

(continued)

(continued)

What if ... ?

Students touch themselves inappropriately during the game?

➤ Some students will touch themselves initially, but most will learn and correct themselves by watching their peers and wanting to be part of the group.

➤ Recap work on private places: ask the student to tell you what room you are working in. Recap which places are private in the school. Establish that the classroom is not a private place.

➤ Can the student recognise and name private body parts? Recap some body parts work. The group needs to have done some prior work on private places and recognising private body parts.

➤ Ask the student to practise 'No, that's private'.

➤ A staff member can stand next to and act as a mirror for the student to copy.

➤ If the student continues to touch him/herself inappropriately ask them to sit and watch the rest of the group and join in later.

Other things you can do

➤ Ask students to make suggestions and lead the rest of the group.

[This activity is amended from *Let's Do It*, Image in Action 1997]

Getting what you want

We all need to know how to be assertive from time to time. Assertion doesn't mean being aggressive, but it does mean being clear about what we want and stating it clearly – if necessary repeating it. These two scenes show the difference when a) Tom does not use the rules, and b) when he does.

➔ Remind students of the *Rules for assertion*.

> ➔ **Decide what you want.**
>
> ➔ **Get the person's attention.**
>
> ➔ **Say what you want clearly and simply.**
>
> ➔ **Keep at it.**

➔ Practise assertive body language.

➔ Show picture 8 and read the story.

➔ Discuss the situation eg is it fair to push in?

➔ Ask students for suggestions about what Tom could do or say.

Here is an example showing how Tom could use the rules:

— … When you push in front of me

— … I feel very upset

— … I would like you to go to your right place in the queue

➔ Role play some of these responses, practising assertive speech and body language.

➔ Show picture 9 and read the text.

Other things you can do

> Teachers can role play some examples of poor responses, exaggerating them for effect.

> Ask students for young people's experiences of not getting what they want. Discuss and role play some appropriate responses. Or staff can think of situations they know present problems for students eg in the lunch queue.

> Use another example eg Debbie returns a damaged tee shirt to a shop.

> Opening lines: students practise using assertive 'opening lines' and continuing the conversation until their request is fulfilled eg: 'I want chips, not baked potato, please', 'My timetable is wrong'.

Getting what you want

Tom in the sandwich bar

Tom is in a sandwich bar. He is waiting in the queue, but someone pushes in front. Tom does not know what to say so he tries to move back in front himself. The man just stands still and ignores Tom. Tom just decides to stay where he is in the queue behind the man.

8

What happens when Tom follows the rules?

Tom is in the sandwich bar waiting in the queue and someone pushes in front. Tom gets into a position where he can see the man's eyes and says in a loud voice but not shouting, 'Excuse me, you have moved in front of me in the queue, I was next.' The man pretends not to notice Tom. Tom steps a little closer and stands straight, again looking directly at the man. He repeats 'I don't think you heard me. I was next in the queue, and you have moved in front of me. I would like you to step back so I can take my proper turn.' The man looks embarrassed and says 'Sorry I didn't see you there. You go next then.'

9

Supporting work to do at home

The stories in this chapter can be retold at home, giving an opportunity to consider situations that might be specific to the local area, or local people. It's a good idea to talk about these things with your son or daughter, so that they can be helped to think about ways of preventing difficulties and the consequences of their actions. Sometimes situations in TV soaps can provide a way into discussing a particular issue.

For instance:

— What do you take with you when you go out?
— Where is a mobile phone carried?
— What arrangements will you make about coming home after college, or a social event?
— Is it sensible to wear such a short skirt? How might other people respond?
— Who would you go to for help if you needed it?

Getting what you want

It can be really helpful to say the assertive lines yourself and ask your son or daughter to repeat them. If you don't mind a bit of acting, then practising them through role play makes it more likely your son or daughter will be able to do it when it's really necessary.

Help your child to be assertive in real situations in their life. Sometimes it may seem easier to answer for him/her or make the decision yourself but this will not help in the long term. We can also face difficulties from other people who do not give your son/daughter the chance or the time or who patronise them. Make it clear from your behaviour that you will give time, respect and proper attention to your child and direct questions to them. This will help others to do the same. If this still doesn't work then we may have to practise the assertive rules ourselves to change the way others behave towards people with disabilities!

Check the stuff

As your teenager becomes more independent he or she will have more 'stuff'.

- **They will want to have their own bag or wallet** so it is worth checking that these are as secure as possible. Maybe you can go out and buy them together and choose secure bags with safe fastenings, explaining why these are most suitable.

- **Telephones can be a big problem**. It's natural for us to want to know quickly if our child needs help. If a mobile is carried it should be well out of sight. An alternative is to provide a phone card for use in a call box. A card with the key numbers of family and friends on it can be kept in a wallet for quick referral.

- **An important sign of independence is having our own door keys**; but if your son or daughter carries them, make sure they have also practised opening the door – or you may find them still on the doorstep when you arrive home!

CHAPTER

3 Relationships

This book is mostly about helping our young people to understand about sexual relationships, which is what chapter 4 is all about. But most of our relationships aren't sexual. They may involve family, social acquaintances, professional encounters, shared work or social activity, liking – even love – but they are not sexual. It's these relationships we explore in this chapter.

Most of us accept without thinking that we behave in different ways with different people, but that's not so easy for our young people who may need a lot of help to appreciate why and how they relate to the many people in their lives, and why they should treat people differently. One of the hardest things for learning disabled people is understanding other people's motives, feelings and responses.

The experiences of Tom and Debbie, once again, are used to illustrate the theme, with their families and friends, and the new people and situations they meet at college. The chapter ends with some material which begins to differentiate between sexual and non-sexual relationships in preparation for chapter 4. We start with an activity which introduces the theme: What are relationships?

The material in this chapter discusses these areas:

> ❸ **appropriate greetings**
>
> ❸ **family and wider relationships**
>
> ❸ **the difference between liking and loving**
>
> ❸ **building a relationship.**

ACTIVITY 1

What are relationships?

You will need a wide range of pictures of male and female people cut out from magazines, including as many differences as you can. Try to find older people and children and people from as many different ethnic groups and cultures as possible. Find pictures of people doing a range of jobs, and include pictures of people with learning disabilities if you can.

Suggestions for classroom work

⊃ Choose about six different pictures and lay them out in front of the students.

⊃ Ask them to tell you about the person in each picture, eg old or young.

⊃ Choose one of the pictures as the main character. Place it in the centre of a table.

⊃ Ask students to make up relationships for that character with the people in the other five pictures. For example: A woman is the main character you have chosen. Which of the people in the other pictures is her partner, her colleague, her niece, her father, her friend, a stranger, the builder, her doctor?

⊃ Now decide how close the relationship is with each of these people. Discuss where to place the pictures, close or far away from the main character, according to the level of the relationship. Her partner could be the closest, the stranger furthest away.

⊃ At the end, remind students that these are just pictures from a magazine, and the relationships are not real. Next time you do the activity they could all be different.

What if ... ?

Students find this too hard?

➤ Use two pictures. Agree on the main character, then ask 'Would this picture of a man be her father or her mother?'

➤ Use only two or three pictures to start with and make the connections yourself eg 'This is her father. This is her niece'.

Students are able to do this easily?

➤ Make up stories for the characters and discuss how the relationships develop (see below).

Other things you can do

➤ Discuss the relationships of the people in the pictures by asking questions like: What does she like about her partner? Who can she talk to most easily – the doctor or her friend?

Family relationships

More members of **Tom** and **Debbie's** families are introduced in some typical family situations. The stories are simple, but they lend themselves to discussing the feelings of the different people involved.

1   Debbie's bedroom

- Show picture 1 (Debbie's bedroom) and read the text.

- Ask students if this is a familiar situation.

- Divide the class into three groups. Ask each group to imagine they are one of the three characters, and talk about how their character is feeling, and why.

- Now ask each group what might be done to improve the situation.

- Show picture 2.

- Ask which of the characters has made the changes happen.

- Show picture 3.

- Ask students to identify what Debbie and Tracey have learnt from their argument.

2   Tom's room

Repeat the work in a similar way for the picture story about Tom.

Other things you can do

This activity can be used to extend work on personal and social skills eg by discussing:

- everyone needs their own space

- people have rights and responsibilities and need to learn to balance these

- siblings should respect each other and their things

- there has to be give and take when people are living together

- difficulties can be sorted out through negotiation and agreement

- families can be places where individual's rights are respected and where everyone can share common interests and have fun together.

Debbie's bedroom

Debbie's bedroom is very untidy. Mum has asked her to clean up the mess. Tracey is standing by the door. She is furious. 'Debbie's been pinching my things' she says crossly. 'She's taken my best tee shirt.' 'Don't shout' says Mum.

1

Debbie tidies her bedroom

2

Mum tells Debbie that she needs to respect Tracey's things and ask if she wants to borrow something. But she also says that Tracey needs to be prepared to share her things sometimes. Mum says that when Debbie has tidied her room, there is a good programme on TV they can all watch together.

Watching TV

Now everything is sorted out upstairs, Mum, Tracey and Debbie have come down to watch TV together. They enjoy being with each other and having a laugh.

3

Tom's room

Dad is standing by the door of Tom's bedroom. Dad says Tom's music is too loud and his room is a mess. 'Clear up these dirty clothes, it's a mess in here!' Tom says 'I like my room the way it is.' Dad tells him if he doesn't clear up the dirty clothes he will have to do his washing himself.

4

5

Tom tidies up

Tom doesn't want to do his own washing so he tidies the dirty clothes into the basket. He likes his clothes to look good and smell clean and fresh. When he has his headphones on he can have the music really loud anyway.

Out for a walk together

Now Tom has sorted out his room he can go out for a walk with Dad, Mike and his dog. They enjoy going to the park together and laugh at the dog's silly tricks.

6

 **Friends**

These stories illustrate some common activities that young people do with their friends, and explore the influence that friends can have.

1 Debbie's friends

⚬ Show picture 7 (Debbie and Karen).

⚬ Ask students where young people meet new friends.

⚬ Show picture 8.

⚬ List all the activities students do with their friends.

⚬ Show picture 9.

⚬ Ask why Karen has started smoking.

⚬ Discuss how Karen's friends might be able to persuade her to stop.

2 Tom's friends

Repeat the work in a similar way for the picture story about Tom.

Other things you can do

Discussion

⚬ **What makes a good friend?**

Using the scenarios in these stories, work can be extended to develop other areas of the personal, social and health education curriculum, for example:

— how to make new friends and welcome new people into a friendship group

— how friends support and value each other

— understanding about healthy lifestyles and that smoking and drinking are bad for health

— understanding pressures that young women come under about their body shape and self-image

— understanding the pressure young people experience to abuse alcohol and the pressure young men are under to appear 'macho'

— how to use peer pressure positively.

Debbie's friends

Debbie and Karen are finding their maths work difficult. Asima offers to help. They don't know her very well, but are grateful when she explains how to do the maths. They all start chatting and arrange to meet up at the weekend.

7

On Saturday, the three young women meet up at the tennis courts in their local park. They enjoy playing together and having a joke too. Debbie says 'Well done Karen, you are better at tennis than you are at maths!'.

8

9

The three friends enjoy a break in the park cafe. Karen explains she is taking up smoking because it will help her to lose weight. Debbie says 'You don't need to lose weight – you look great!' Asima agrees and says 'All this exercise will keep you fit and looking good – don't spoil it by doing something so unhealthy. If my parents found out I was smoking they would be really angry.'

Tom and Jake are cheering as Manjit plays basketball. He is playing really well and scores for his team to win. His friends are proud of him and happy for his success.

10

11

After the basketball match, they meet up in the pub. Brad is already there and has drunk three pints. He is smoking. 'Why didn't you come to the game?' asks Tom, 'Manjit was brilliant.' 'I needed a cigarette and a drink after my lousy day' complains Brad. 'Don't always think about yourself' says Jake, 'you should give those cigarettes up – no one likes kissing a bloke who stinks of fags.'

They all play pool. Brad says 'At least let me buy you all a drink – pints all round?' Tom says he will have a bottle of beer and Manjit and Jake both choose fruit juice. 'You lot aren't much fun' says Brad. 'You don't have to get drunk to have a good time' says Jake.

12

Relationships with teachers

These stories indicate the appropriate relationship between students and their teachers. The issue of homosexual relationships is mentioned in passing, and there is an opportunity to consider what are the acceptable boundaries of relationships between older and younger people.

- Show picture 13 (Tom).

- Ask students why Tom might be worried about asking his teacher for help.

- Ask students for other situations where they might have to ask a teacher or another adult for help. They can role play these situations, practising appropriate language.

- Show picture 14 (Debbie).

- Karen fancies her teacher. Why does Debbie think it's not OK?

- Use the activity 'Who do they fancy?' (p 52) to discuss appropriate age differences in relationships.

- Use this opportunity to raise the issue of same sex relationships, and to reassure that it's OK for people to fancy someone of the same sex and to choose to be with them.

Other things you can do

Use this material to discuss these points:

- Knowing that it is OK not to understand something and that it is OK to ask. People with learning disabilities have a right to good service.

- Learning effective ways of asking for something.

- Making choices is part of adult life – food, where to sit, who to fancy.

- Young women may be lesbian or bisexual and young men may be gay or bisexual. This is OK.

- Young people may be exploring their sexuality and have crushes on older people of either sex.

- It is important to know about socially acceptable behaviour and that it is more common for young people to go out with people of their own age.

- Be aware of exploitation of young people by older adults.

- Be aware of appropriate boundaries between young people and professionals they may get to know eg teachers, social workers etc.

Relationships with teachers

In the computer class

Tom is in the computer class. He doesn't understand something on his screen. He is worried about asking the teacher about it. Eventually he says 'Excuse me, can you help me, I'm a bit stuck.' Derek Hopkins says 'Well done Tom, I'm glad you asked. I'm here to help you learn. What is it you don't understand?' and he explains it clearly to Tom.

13

In the canteen

14

Debbie and Karen have chosen their lunch from the canteen menu and paid at the till. They are looking for somewhere to sit. Karen says 'Let's go and sit by Miss Foster, I think she's gorgeous.'

'You don't fancy her do you? She's a woman' says Debbie. 'I might do' says Karen. 'It's OK for girls to fancy other girls.' 'That may be true' says Debbie 'but she's years older than you and anyway she's a teacher.'

ACTIVITY 5

Tom talks to strangers

This activity raises issues about appropriate ways of talking to the people that Tom might meet during a typical day.

> Enlarge the pictures of the heads separately and cut them out. Use a picture of Tom (from chapter 1). Set the scene for scene 1.

> Read text a) with two adults taking the parts if possible. Ask students if this is OK.

> Ask students to suggest more appropriate words to use in the situation.

> Read text b).

> Continue in a similar way with the other scenes.

> Students will enjoy role playing these or other situations that they identify. (It's a good idea to get staff members to role play the 'wrong' responses, and students to try out the 'right' ones, to avoid confusion).

People Tom meets

15

The scenes

— Tom with the bus driver
— Tom at the Post Office counter
— Tom meets the college principal
— Tom and a stranger at bus stop
— Tom and the college receptionist

On the bus

a) 'I've always wanted to be a bus driver. Can I sit in your seat?', (pulling at the driver's arm)

b) 'A ticket to the town centre please.'

At the Post Office

a) 'I'll give you a present of £10.00.'

b) 'Here is my book. I want to put £10.00 in the post office please.'

The college principal

a) 'Can you give me a lift home?'

b) 'Yes, I am enjoying my course, thank you.'

At the bus stop

a) 'Hello I'm Tom. I'd like one of those sweets.' (hugging stranger)

b) 'Is another bus due soon?'

The college receptionist

a) 'Will you be my girlfriend?'

b) 'Can you tell me the way to room 19 please?'

Other things you can do

Do more work on these areas:

- body language, appropriate phrases

- assertion skills

- who is who and how to address them appropriately

- different levels of intimacy

- people have different roles in relation to the individual

If your students find these too obvious:

- use more sophisticated but still inappropriate responses eg
  'I bet you earn a lot of money' (to college principal)
  'Fancy coming down to the pub at lunchtime?' (to the receptionist)
  'Nice clothes you've got' (at the bus stop)

Relationship circles

This is a way of helping to sort out the many different relationships we experience in our lives, using Tom and Debbie as our examples. This is also an activity that families can do at home, using the young person's real circle of relationships.

→ Make a list with students of all the people Tom knows. Add one or two more family members and teachers. You can photocopy p 45 and cut out the individual characters.

→ Draw a small circle containing Tom's picture in the middle of a large sheet of paper.

→ Ask students which of the people on the list are members of Tom's family.

→ Place these people around Tom to show how close students think they are to him.

→ Continue in the same way with Tom's friends, and then his teachers and other adults.

→ Discuss how Tom's feelings about people may be different depending how close or far they are from him on the chart.

→ Discuss whether degree of closeness may change over time. For example, Debbie later becomes Tom's girlfriend.

Repeat the process for Debbie's relationships.

Other things you can do

→ Students can choose pictures from magazines to add to Tom and Debbie's circles. They can invent characters for them.

→ Draw chalk circles on the floor and place students to represent Tom and Debbie's relationships. In this case, it's important to label the students well, either by holding big names, or holding pictures of the characters or by wearing masks.

Tom's Dad

Mike

Tom's Mum

Manjit

TOM

Tom's Nan

Bus driver

Debbie

Jake

Post Office
counter worker

Doctor

Derek Hopkins
Computer teacher

Debbie's Mum

Tracey

Debbie's Grandpa

Doctor

Debbie's Grandma

Asima

DEBBIE

Cousin Jack

Karen

Tom

Canteen staff

Cathy Foster
Drama teacher

Manjit

Derek Hopkins
Computer teacher

Liking and loving

This is an exercise to identify the differences in feelings for other people, especially the difference between liking and loving.

> You will need:

> — A large sheet of paper with a straight line drawn across it.
> — Pictures of people in Tom and Debbie's circles of relationships (you can enlarge and cut out the people in Tom and Debbie's circles of relationships in the previous activity).

> Write 'LIKE' at one end of the line and 'LOVE' at the other.

> Start with either Tom or Debbie. Choose one picture from their circle.

> Number students around the group. Ask the first student to place the picture where s/he thinks it should go on the line.

> Continue with further pictures and students in turn.

> When all the pictures have been placed, ask students (perhaps in pairs) whether they agree with the positions. Ask them to say why they agree or disagree.

> In the discussion, explore what students think is the difference between liking and loving. And is loving your mother the same as loving your boy or girlfriend?

This activity can be repeated using pictures of people we know of but don't know personally; eg pop stars, politicians, TV characters.

> Where would students place them on a liking/loving line?

> Or on a liking/disliking line?

Supporting work to do at home

A relationship circle

Make a relationship circle for your child. Remember it can change as they grow up. This can help your son or daughter understand some of the differences between different relationships in their lives.

- Make a list with your son or daughter of all the people they know.

- Draw a small circle in the middle of a large sheet of paper and write your child's name in it, or even better, put a photograph of him or her in it.

- Place pictures of members of your family around your son or daughter on the sheet to show how close s/he thinks they are to him/her.

- Continue in the same way with photos, drawings or written names of friends, and then teachers and other adults.

- Discuss how your child's feelings about people may be different depending how close or far they are on the chart.

- Discuss whether the degree of closeness may change over time. For example, a stranger may become a girl/boyfriend or partner; cousins may not have anything in common once they grow up.

Liking and loving

An exercise to identify the differences in feelings for other people, especially the difference between liking and loving.

- You will need:
  - A large sheet of paper with a straight line drawn across it.
  - Pictures of people in the relationship circle you have made in the activity above.

- Write 'LIKE' at one end of the line and 'LOVE' at the other.

- Choose one picture from their circle.

- Ask your child to place the picture where s/he thinks it should go on the line.

- Continue with further pictures.

- When all the pictures have been placed, you can talk about why the pictures have been placed in those positions.

- The discussion can explore the difference between liking and loving. Is loving your mother the same as loving your boy or girlfriend?

All about sex

Sex is everywhere – in advertisements (think about ads for new cars!), in magazines, on TV. Pressures on young people to exhibit their growing sexuality are hard for them to resist.

In our society, sexual behaviour has changed. The issue is no longer about whether sex before marriage should or should not take place, when casual sex, several partners and long term partnership without marriage are not unusual for younger age groups. But official policies, and some people's views, hardly acknowledge these changes, making it difficult for us to know what to teach our students.

School sex and relationships education can be hedged about with caveats and restrictions, making it hard for us to adopt an honest and open approach. Sex and relationships education is seen by some as encouraging young people to have sex, so that schools are hesitant about talking explicitly about some vital health issues, like HIV, where infection rates among heterosexuals have been growing fast in recent years. The same hesitancy prevents any open discussion about homosexuality, an omission that does nothing to deter the homophobia which is revealed in playgrounds as well as in wider society.

How are we to help our learning disabled students to make sense of all this? They are likely to be even more confused than their mainstream peers, and undoubtedly more vulnerable. There is a dilemma here. If our students are to learn effectively, they need more sex and relationships education with more explicit materials than students in mainstream schools; yet there are still those who believe that sex and relationships education and a sexual life are not appropriate for people with disabilities and disapprove of the materials that would be most useful. There is another problem with explicit visual materials: not all of us as parents or teachers feel comfortable with them ourselves and cannot be comfortable with them at home or in the classroom. This is good reason for providing sex and relationships education at school, and for making sure that only people trained and at ease with the subject are teaching it.

We want our young people to grow up with confidence, to love and be loved, to live life to the full, yet without being exploited or damaged. Is this possible? The writers have wide experience of providing effective sex and relationships education courses for young people and adults with learning disabilities, using similar material to that in this chapter. We know that a factual and straightforward approach is necessary, with very clear and unambiguous illustrations. This is what we provide here.

The materials in this chapter discuss these areas/issues:

> **⊃** **sex in the context of a loving relationship**
>
> **⊃** **safer sex practices**
>
> **⊃** **the role of the family**
>
> **⊃** **using the family planning clinic.**

These episodes continue to follow the fortunes of Tom and Debbie, who are both 18+, until they eventually have sex together, as part of a longer term relationship. To fit with your school's policy on sex and relationships education, and the particular religious and cultural mix of your students, you can make changes to the stories, to the length of the relationship, to an engagement or marriage process for instance.

Another possibility is to introduce a story about Asima, one of Debbie's friends, with her different family and cultural background and her experience of a developing sexual relationship.

We suggest you read the story as you show the pictures, and then use one or more of the activities to take the work in the direction most appropriate for your group.

Episode 1: When it all started

Tom and Debbie meet at college

Tom is in the computer class, working at his desk. He is feeling a bit shy.

Debbie has lots of friends. She is working at her desk and laughing with her friend Karen.

Debbie notices Tom. She thinks he looks nice. She asks her friend Karen 'Who's he? He's new here. I like the look of him.'

Tom looks at Debbie and Karen. He wonders if they are laughing at him. Tom thinks Debbie looks nice. He wants to go and speak to her but he is too shy.

On the way home: 1

It's time to go home. Debbie gets her bag. She sits on the bus and thinks about the new boy. She hopes she will see him again.

On the way home: 2

Tom walks home. He thinks about the girl with the green top. He hopes he will see her again. He wonders what her name is. He wonders if she has a boyfriend.

Who do they fancy?

Use a selection of pictures of different individuals cut out from magazines with a range of age, gender, race etc.

❯ Place the pictures on a table or the floor.

❯ Ask students to decide which two of the people in the photographs may 'fancy' one another (male/female; male/male; female/female).

❯ Ask why these two people might fancy one another.

❯ Ask students what might interest Tom about Debbie, and Debbie about Tom.

❯ Discuss/make a list of things that attract people to one another.

❯ This is another opportunity to discuss homosexuality. Students can be reassured that it's OK to be gay, and that some people choose partners of the same sex.

[This activity is amended from *Let's Do It*, Image in Action 1997]

Episode 2: The following week

Tom and Debbie meet again

4

Tom is waiting for the computer class to start. Debbie is sitting at her desk. They keep looking at one other. 'Do you want a sweet?' asks Tom. 'Yes' says Debbie, 'What's your name?'

'Tom' says Tom, 'What's yours?' 'Debbie' says Debbie, chewing her sweet. Debbie goes back to her desk.

Now when they look at each other they smile. At the end of the lesson Debbie asks Tom if he is going to the canteen. 'Maybe we could have a coffee together?' They go off happily. They enjoy their chat and agree to meet at the youth club.

Tom and Debbie become close friends

5

Debbie and Tom spend a lot of time together at college. They hold hands whenever they can. They want to sit together, they want to be close all the time. 'You are my girlfriend' says Tom. Debbie says 'I'm not sure my mum wants me to have a boyfriend.'

Whenever their teacher sees them she says 'Stop all this touching. This is not a private place.'

ACTIVITY 1 : First lines

❯ Ask students to suggest possible 'first lines' when Tom and Debbie talk to one another for the first time.

❯ Role play the meeting using different first lines so that students can practise them and see how well they work.

❯ Role play the conversation in the canteen.

ACTIVITY 2 : Stepping stones

❯ Draw some stepping stones on a large sheet of paper or board. Write 'classroom' on the first stone and then arrow to the next. Write 'canteen' on the next stone.

❯ Ask students where they think the next meeting might be. Write the agreed place on the next stone.

❯ Ask for ideas about what Tom and Debbie might talk about/do at this meeting.

❯ Role play the meeting, using different versions of the conversation.

Other things you can do

❯ A more active activity: you can place large hoops on the floor as stepping stones and use pictures of the characters. Meetings can be role played in or beside these hoops.

❯ If you are telling the story of Asima, you can make a separate set of stepping stones for her experiences.

Tom visits Debbie's mum

6

One Saturday afternoon Tom goes to have tea with Debbie's family. Debbie waves at him from the window. She has been watching for him coming. She opens the door. She wants to give him a hug and a kiss but her mum is right behind her.

'Hello Mrs P' mumbles Tom.

'Hello Tom. I'm Debbie's mum. You can call me Liz. Come in, I've been wanting to meet you.'

'Put the kettle on, Debbie' says Liz. 'Sit down Tom and tell me how you like college.'

'I'm really enjoying my computer course and I like the pizza at lunch times,' says Tom. 'Debbie talks about you a lot. She says you are her boyfriend' says Liz. 'Yes I like having Debbie as my girlfriend, she's great fun' says Tom.

'Well, you seem like a nice young man, but I worry about Debbie and I don't want anyone messing around with her. Do you understand what I am saying?'

Debbie comes in with the tea and some cake. They all eat the cake and chat until it is time to go. When her mum has gone back into the kitchen, Debbie gives Tom a quick hug and kiss. 'See you tomorrow' she says.

Why is Mum anxious?

> Ask students for reasons why Debbie's mum might be anxious about Tom and Debbie.

> Then ask them to think of things that might make her less anxious.

> Ask students if they think Tom understands what 'messing around' with Debbie means.

Tom and Debbie enjoy spending time together and getting to know each other. They go out to the youth club and the cinema. They like going for walks in the park and Debbie persuades Tom to take up tennis. Sometimes they go to the local disco with their friends. They help each other with their college work. They also look after each other when things go wrong: when Debbie got bad marks in her maths test or when Tom lost his file and Debbie spent all her lunch hour helping him look for it.

7

8

They get to know one another's families. Debbie likes animals and enjoys walking Mike's dog. Tom helps Tracey with her work on the computer and helps to wash Liz's car.

They enjoy being physically close. They hold hands and hug and kiss one another. Their families call them the 'lovebirds'.

Stepping stones *(continued)*

- ➔ Make a list of activities that can be done locally by young people, with a partner or with a group.

- ➔ Ask for suggestions about what the next step in Tom and Debbie's relationship might be.

- ➔ Continue to add steps to the relationship of Tom and Debbie.

Other things you can do

- ➔ Place pictures of local places or situations around Tom and Debbie.

- ➔ You can alter the story to fit the sort of activities your students take part in (within reason!). The story is suitable for students with severe learning disabilities but alterations may be made to make it more appropriate for those with more moderate disabilities.

- ➔ Continue with Asima's stepping stones if you are telling her story.

Episode 5: Debbie and Tom alone

On the sofa

Debbie and Tom are boyfriend and girlfriend. They have been boyfriend and girlfriend for three months now. Debbie's mum is still at work. Tom has come round to Debbie's house. They are alone.

They sit and watch the TV together. They sit very close. Tom puts his arm around Debbie. She puts her hand on his leg. They are happy together. They feel relaxed.

Tom tells Debbie he wants to kiss her. Debbie turns to him and says yes she would like to kiss him too. They start kissing. They kiss slowly. It feels good. They stop watching the TV. They start to touch one another's bodies over their clothes. It feels exciting to be so close.

Liz comes in unexpectedly

Suddenly the door bangs. They jump apart. 'Hello love' calls out Debbie's mum. She comes into the sitting room. 'What have you been up to then?' she asks. 'Watching TV!' say Tom and Debbie together.

TALKING TOGETHER…ABOUT SEX AND RELATIONSHIPS • fpa   **59**

ACTIVITY 1 — What are they feeling?

- Invite suggestions about what Tom and Debbie feel when Liz comes in.

- Do the same for ideas about how Liz feels when she sees the two of them together.

ACTIVITY 2 — Privacy

- Ask students to identify appropriate private places for intimate behaviour.

- Make a list of ways of expressing sexual feeling eg a short kiss, a long kiss, big hug, touching private parts of their bodies through clothes, holding hands, taking off clothes.

- Match each expression of feeling to the appropriate place – public or private.

ACTIVITY 3 Sex is about ...

If students' reading ability is sufficient, give each one a copy of Activity Sheet 1 on p 62. Ask them to do one of the following:

— to mark each statement with a tick or cross

— to mark the three most important

This can also be done in pairs or small groups.

Then go through the statements and discuss what marks the students have given.

If reading ability is poorer, read out each statement separately and discuss how true it is.

Other things you can do

If students find it too complicated to use the list in this way, you can use pictures instead. Use pictures cut out from magazines, or some of the later pictures in this book, to show different aspects of sex and sexual feelings.

Choose THREE things from the list which best show what sex is about.

1	Being in love
2	Having children
3	Caring for someone else
4	Fancying someone
5	Feeling nervous
6	Intercourse
7	Kissing
8	Fun
9	Looking into someone's eyes
10	Using condoms
11	Holding hands
12	Being able to talk
13	Catching infections
14	
15	

Episode 6: Feeling sexy – 1

Debbie and Tom alone

11

Debbie and Tom are alone in her bedroom. Her mum is at work. They have some private time together. They sit together very close with their arms around each other. It feels good to be alone. They feel happy and relaxed.

Getting sexy

12

They squeeze each other close and kiss for a long time. They feel sexy being together. Debbie can feel her heart beating. Tom can feel his penis start to go hard. He has an erection. They start to touch each other's private parts and take off some clothes.

Tom touches Debbie's breasts. Debbie touches Tom's bottom. Tom starts to touch Debbie's private parts. 'Do you like this?' he asks. 'Yes' says Debbie. They both are feeling very sexy. Their breathing is getting faster and deeper.

Episode 6: Feeling sexy – 2

No sex without a condom

'I love you' says Tom. 'I love you too' says Debbie. Tom really wants to have sex. 'I'd like to make love with you' he says. 'I want to too, but have you got a condom?' says Debbie.

'No' says Tom. He is disappointed. 'Haven't you got one?' he asks. 'No' says Debbie.

13

They look at one another. They both want to have sex but they both know that sex without a condom is very risky.

What can they do? Debbie and Tom know they can't have sex without a condom.

'Oh, let's just do it' says Tom 'You won't get pregnant and we haven't got any disease.'

'Are you crazy?' says Debbie. She is angry. 'How do you know? I didn't see you last night. How do I know that you didn't have sex with someone else?'

14

'But I love you' says Tom 'You can trust me.'

'I do trust you' says Debbie 'but we can't make love without a condom.'

Tom leaves

'I'd better go', says Tom. He gets dressed. 'I think we should talk about this some more because I really love you and want to be with you.'

Debbie feels upset but she says 'Yes. Anyway, see you at college tomorrow.'

Sex: yes or no?

● Enlarge and cut out the statements on Activity Sheet 2 separately. It's best to use card.

● Hold up and read out one card at a time. Ask students to raise their hands to show whether they think it is a good reason for Tom and Debbie to have sex, or a reason for them NOT to have sex.

● Place each card on the pile students have voted for: good reason, or not.

● In the whole group, or in small groups, each statement can be discussed eg:

— Why was it placed on that pile?

— Do all students agree with the placing?

— Might other people have different views?

● Students can make other suggestions to add to the list.

Other things you can do

Ask students to place the cards on a continuum line between 'good' and 'bad' reasons. This is slightly more sophisticated and will allow more differentiated views to appear.

ACTIVITY SHEET 2: Sex: yes or no?

Here are some reasons why Tom and Debbie should, or should not, have sex.

They are over 16	**Everyone on TV does it**
They have known one another a short time	**They love one another**
They fancy one another	**They are in a private place**
They trust one another	**All their friends are doing it**
This is what they want to do	**They haven't got a condom**
They aren't married	**Their parents wouldn't want them to**

ACTIVITY 2

Talking about condoms

People think everything to do with sex should be spontaneous which makes talking about planning to have sex and obtaining contraceptives difficult. This activity gives a chance to practise some 'spontaneous' lines before the event!

- ➤ Ask students why people find it difficult to talk about contraception (or using condoms).

- ➤ Use the drawings of Tom and Debbie in their underwear (see pp 9 and 11) to read the opening lines below, and to continue the conversations.

- ➤ Students can discuss which lines might work best.

    'I love you and I want it to be right. Shall we buy some condoms?'

    'Let's make it special, I don't want to rush it now. I want to feel safe. I don't want a baby.'

    'Let's wait until we are ready.' 'I am ready.'
    'Have you got any condoms?' 'No.'
    'Well, you're not ready then!'

    'I bought a condom in case we want to go the whole way. I want us to feel relaxed and safe.'

Other things you can do

- ➤ Discuss with students where condoms can be acquired eg:

    — bought from a shop or a vending machine

    — free from a family planning clinic.

- ➤ Set up a role play in a pharmacy and use the drawings of Tom and Debbie clothed (pp 8 and 10) buying condoms.

- ➤ If appropriate, plan a visit to a local pharmacy to look at toiletries on sale, including condoms.

Further information

FACTSHEET 1:   Sex and the law

FACTSHEET 1: Sex and the law

Most people with learning disabilities have the same rights and protection in law as everybody else. This means that they have the right to:

- ➲ Receive **sex and relationships education**.

- ➲ Decide about their own **medical treatment** once they are 16. *Even those under 16 can sometimes decide by themselves.*

- ➲ Consent to **sexual activity** once they are 16 (17 in Northern Ireland). This is the same for men and women, and for heterosexual (straight) and homosexual (gay) sex. *People under 16 (17 in Northern Ireland) cannot consent to any sexual activity and their partners would be breaking the law.*

- ➲ Use **sexual health services** and know they are confidential, even if under 16. However, staff may involve other services if they believe the young person, or another person, to be at significant risk of harm (for example, physical or sexual abuse). They will discuss this with the young person.

- ➲ Get married or register for a civil partnership (same sex couples) once they are 16. In Scotland, people under 18 do not need parental consent. In England, Wales and Northern Ireland, parental consent is needed until the age of 18. *The registrar has to be sure that people getting married understand what they are doing.*

- ➲ Have legal action taken against anybody who **assaults or rapes** them.

Consent to sexual activity

One of the rights of people with learning disabilities recognised by the United Nations is 'the right to love and be loved … including sexual fulfilment' (Declaration of the Rights of Mentally Handicapped People, 1971). This right is acknowledged and supported by social, education and health services. In practice, sexual activity between consenting learning disabled adults is not now considered a matter for the law, although a clause in an Act of 1956 says otherwise, and there is no legal responsibility to report sexual activity between two learning disabled people, if both are happy about it.

At issue is the ability or otherwise of either party to consent. The Mental Capacity Act 2005 (to be implemented in 2007) clarified this issue for people with learning disabilities. It states that:

(continued)

- every adult is to be presumed to have capacity unless proven otherwise

- people should be supported to make their own decisions

- people have the right to make what might be seen as eccentric or unwise decisions

- intervention should be the least restrictive possible.

The Act provides a framework to empower and protect vulnerable people who are not able to make their own decisions (have capacity). It provides for a new Court of Protection as the final arbiter of decisions; and a Public Guardian who supervises court approved deputies.

Consent to medical treatment

If someone cannot make a decision for themselves, for example about taking the contraceptive pill or a contraceptive injection, then a doctor can decide to give the treatment to that person if it is in his or her best interests. If the treatment is serious or permanent (such as abortion or sterilisation), and/or there is disagreement about it, then a court will decide if it should go ahead. If the person is capable of understanding what the treatment is then he or she must agree to it him/herself.

Further information

To find out more about existing legislation, and any proposed future legislation, see **www.homeoffice.gov.uk**.

At a party

Debbie is telling Tom how special he is to her. She admires him like no one else.
He is a great dancer and she really fancies him. She really would like to have sex with him. Tom says 'I want that too but I want it to be right for us both. I'm sorry about the other night. I didn't think about a condom.' Debbie says it is a responsibility for both of them and she will ask her sister Tracey about it.

15

Finding the clinic

16

Debbie and Tracey are on their way home from town after shopping. 'There's the family planning clinic' says Tracey. 'You could go to our doctor but the clinic has a session especially for young people on Tuesday afternoon. Why don't you and Tom go together? They're very friendly.' Debbie says she will ask Tom. 'Are you going to tell Mum?' asks Tracey. 'I suppose so' says Debbie 'but I'm a bit embarrassed.' 'I think Mum would be OK about it' says Tracey.

Talking to Mum

Mum is pleased Tom and Debbie are planning to use contraception. She doesn't want Debbie to get pregnant. 'I like Tom and I know how much you mean to each other. It's important that you are in private when you want have sex together and you only do what you want to do. Just ask me if you have any questions. I think you are both being very grown up, I am proud of you.'

Tom and Debbie at the clinic

The doctor is kind and helpful. She asks them what they know about having sex and contraception. They talk about the sex and relationships education lessons they have had at school and college. The doctor shows them a sex and relationships education book. It shows a couple having sex. The man is touching the woman's breasts and clitoris. The woman is touching the man's penis and testicles. The couple in the book put a condom on the man's penis and he puts his penis into the woman's vagina. They both have an orgasm. The man's semen is in the condom and not in the woman's vagina.

19

These pictures show what happens when a man and a woman decide to have sex.

Illustration 1:

Matt and Jessica are in love. They decide to have sex.

Illustration 2:

They are in a private room and will be undisturbed. They both take off their clothes.

Illustration 3:

Matt and Jessica both feel sexy and are touching private parts. Jessica touches Matt's penis and testicles. Matt touches Jessica's breasts and clitoris.

Illustration 4:

Matt gets an erection. He puts a condom on his hard penis so his semen will stay in the condom and not go into Jessica's vagina. This means she will not get pregnant and they will both stay healthy and will not catch infections.

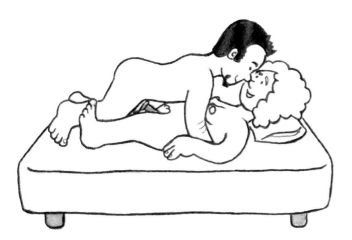

Illustration 5:

Matt has the condom on his penis which he puts in Jessica's vagina. They both feel sexy and excited. Jessica has an orgasm and then Matt has an orgasm. Matt's semen has come out of the end of his penis into the condom.

Illustration 6:

Matt carefully takes his penis out of Jessica's vagina, holding it so that none of the semen comes out. He wraps the condom in a tissue and puts it in the bin. They cuddle and feel happy and contented together.

How to use a condom

74

20

Tom and Debbie look at a packet of condoms. The doctor shows them the condom when it comes out of its packet. She tells them how to see the right way to put it on the penis and roll it down all the way. She encourages Tom and Debbie to practise on the model. She then shows them how to take it off carefully after the man has had an orgasm and it is filled with semen, how to wrap it up and put it in the bin.

The doctor answers all their questions. Tom and Debbie feel relieved and happy that they are prepared for sex when the time is right.

Tom and Debbie ask questions

What if Debbie or Tom doesn't understand something? It is important that they understand so they can make choices and look after themselves. If they don't understand then they can ask questions and tell the staff if they need more help. They have a right to information.

➋ Tom and Debbie ask the doctor some questions:

— **Will it hurt?** (Debbie)

— **Will I wee myself?** (Tom)

➋ Ask students what other questions they think Tom and Debbie might want to ask. (This gives students a chance to find out things they might want to know without admitting their own ignorance or misunderstandings.)

How does Debbie tell her mum?

➋ Invite ideas from students about what Debbie might say to her mum about going to the clinic.

➋ Use role play to explore the conversations that might take place with each of these suggestions.

About contraceptives

This activity will need a set of contraceptives. A *Contraceptive display kit* is available to buy from fpa, and some health promotion units may have one available for loan or hire. This activity will also require a set of unclothed body outlines (such as those in *Talking together... about growing up*) and Factsheet 2 on contraception.

> Show each contraceptive in turn.

> Place it in the correct place on the appropriate body outline, or ask students to do so.

> Clarify by asking students, or by explaining: eg

— who uses each one

— how it works

— when it is used

— where to get it

NOTE: In rural areas the local general practice may be the only source of advice about contraceptives. Make sure students understand about confidentiality.

Further information

ACTIVITY SHEET 3:   **Using a male condom**

FACTSHEET 2:   **Contraception**

Talking together... about contraception, **fpa** 2005.

ACTIVITY SHEET 3: Using a male condom

- Do not let the man's penis get close to his partner's genital area without a condom on.

- Check the use by date on the condom packet.

- Open the packet carefully and take out the condom. Be careful not to tear the condom on rings or sharp fingernails.

- Only put the condom on when the man's penis is hard and erect.

- Make sure the condom is the right way round. Do this before putting the condom on. It needs to unroll easily, but do not unroll it until it is being placed on the penis.

- Squeeze the closed end or the teat of the condom to get rid of any air and put it on the end of the penis.

- Roll the condom right down to the base of the penis. If it won't unroll that far, it's probably on inside out. If so, start again with a new one as sperm may now be on the outside of the condom.

- It is now safe to have sex, but make sure the condom does not come off.

- Take the penis out of the woman's vagina as soon as the man has had an orgasm ('come'), before the penis goes soft. He must hold the condom in place to make sure it does not come off his penis.

- Now take the condom off and wrap it in a tissue.

- Throw the used condom in the bin. Never put it in the toilet.

- Use a new condom every time.

There are many methods of contraception and different methods suit different people. Contraception works mainly by stopping the ovaries from releasing an egg or preventing the sperm and egg from meeting.

When used correctly, contraception is very effective, though no method is 100 per cent. There are some methods with no-user failure, which don't depend on a woman or man remembering to take or use contraception, such as the contraceptive injection, implant, IUS or IUD. Other methods depend on the user thinking about them each day, or at a regular time or each time they have sex, such as the contraceptive pill, the contraceptive patch, the diaphragm or condom.

Male and female condoms offer the best protection against sexually transmitted infections. Diaphragms and caps can offer some protection.

Where to get contraception

Free contraception, including emergency contraception, can be obtained from:

- a general practice, unless they say they don't provide contraception services – ask the doctor or practice nurse

- a contraception (family planning) clinic

- a sexual health clinic

- a young people's service (these will have an upper age limit)

- some genitourinary medicine (GUM) clinics.

Contraception is free even if the service gives a prescription to take to the pharmacy.

Under 16s

Doctors and other health professionals can provide contraceptive advice and treatment to under 16s without their parents' consent if they believe:

- that the young person understands the advice and has sufficient maturity to understand what is involved

(continued)

- they cannot persuade the young person to inform their parents

- the young person would be very likely to begin or continue having sex without contraception

- that without contraceptive advice or treatment the young person's physical or mental health would suffer

- that it would be in the young person's best interests not to inform their parents.

People with learning disabilities

The legal position for people with learning disabilities is the same as for others, including under 16s. Women with learning disabilities cannot be given contraception without their knowledge and consent if they are capable of understanding what it is.

Emergency contraception

Emergency contraception is available for women who have had sex without using contraception, or think their method might have failed. There are two methods:

- The emergency pill must be taken up to three days (72 hours) after sex. It is more effective the earlier it is taken.

- An IUD must be fitted up to five days after sex, or up to five days after the earliest time a woman could have released an egg (ovulation).

Free emergency contraception can be obtained from:

- a general practice, unless they say they don't provide contraception services – ask the doctor or practice nurse

- a contraception (family planning) clinic

- a sexual health clinic

(continued)

- ➔ a young people's service (these will have an upper age limit)

- ➔ some genitourinary medicine (GUM) clinics

- ➔ most NHS walk-in centres (England only) and minor injuries units

- ➔ some hospital accident and emergency departments (phone first to check)

- ➔ some pharmacies (there may be an age limit).

Women aged 16 and over can buy the emergency pill from most pharmacies for around £26.

Further information

fpa offers information and advice on contraception and has a wide range of leaflets. (See useful contacts p 119.)

Under the duvet

21

Debbie tells Tom that it is nice to be together like this. 'I'm glad we waited till the right time to make love' she says. 'And the condom was easier to use than I thought.'

'You are lovely' says Tom. 'I'm so glad you are my girlfriend. I feel great when I am with you.'

'You are very special to me, Tom' says Debbie as they cuddle happily together.

Introductory work

⊃ Make sure students know about sexual body parts and functions. Use pictures or diagrams to clarify them. The body outlines in *Talking together… about growing up* can be used for this.

⊃ Use an activity like Pass the Condom (in *Let's Do It* see Useful resources) to familiarise students with handling a condom.

⊃ Use a penis model to demonstrate ejaculation of semen (often available from your local health promotion unit).

Using a condom

> You will need:
>
> — a model penis (preferably one which can ejaculate synthetic semen)
>
> — a packet of condoms
>
> — one or more copies of Activity Sheet 3: *Using a male condom*.
>
> It would also be helpful to have copies of leaflets from **fpa** on using a condom. *Talking together ... about contraception* includes a useful section on using a condom, with clear illustrations.

How to do it

> Demonstrate placing a condom on the penis model, ensuring that the steps in the activity sheet *Using a male condom* are followed.

> Make the penis model ejaculate into the condom (this may need some advance practice!)

> **Either:** give out copies of the activity sheet (if reading ability is sufficient) and talk students through it stage by stage, repeating each stage with the model
>
> **or:** ask students to identify the stages in using a condom, and repeat each stage on the model, using a fresh condom
>
> **or:** another adult can read the activity sheet aloud while you demonstrate with the penis model.

Other things you can do

If an ejaculating penis is hard to locate, or difficult to use, adapt the activity to using a non-ejaculating one.

Supporting work to do at home

Episodes 1 and 2

In your family, who is attracted to who? Who are the couples (eg uncle and aunt)?

- Arrange photos of the couples together.

- Ask your son or daughter what they think are the characteristics that attracted them to one another? Include physical characteristics.

- What do the couples have in common? (discuss, or make a list) eg common interests, similar social context, religious or cultural similarities, views, principles, politics.

- How did the couples meet? Was it at work, playing sport, at a club?

To think about …

Do you have views about the kind of person you would like your son or daughter to have a relationship with? Is your culture one that organises events where young people can meet? Are the families normally involved in supporting meetings between young people? Will it be the same for your child with a learning disability?

Episode 3

Using the story in episode 3:

- Think about situations that would make you anxious for your son or daughter. You can talk about this with your partner or a friend.

- Use this opportunity to talk to your son or daughter about your anxieties. Does s/he understand what Debbie's mother means when she says 'I don't want anyone messing about with her?'

Episode 4

- What are the options for young people to do in your locality? Is there a local youth club or organisation providing activities for young people with disabilities? Can you get together with other parents to plan alternatives for your children?

Episode 5

- Think about which spaces in your home are private. Discuss this with your son or daughter. Where would it be appropriate for them to be in private with a friend?

(continued)

- Suggest your son or daughter makes or buys a name plate for their door with 'Keep out. Private!' or 'Please knock before entering'.

- Is it always possible to respect this privacy? What are your concerns or reasons for this? You can talk about this with your son or daughter.

- How would you face the situation in the story? Would you say anything eg about privacy, about arranging for the two families to meet so that they can agree how to support the young people?

Episode 6

Many parents never have to face the reality of their children having sex. Maybe it will help to think about which aspects we can deal with, and where we might get help or support if necessary. Find out if there is a local group for parents of teenagers to talk about these matters. Is there any professional support available? There may be a school nurse or counsellor you could talk to.

You could plan a visit to a local pharmacy to familiarise your son or daughter with various toiletries on sale, including condoms.

Episode 7

- You can tell this story to introduce the subject of contraception. You can explain your family's attitude to it, and any religious views you may have. *Talking together ... about contraception* has ideas and advice for discussing these topics.

- Find out where the local family planning clinic is and whether they have sessions for young people. You can get details of clinics from **fpa** (on 0845 122 8690 or at www.fpa.org.uk); NHS direct at www.nhs.direct.nhs.uk – in England and Wales you can call NHS Direct on 0845 46 47, in Scotland NHS 24 on 08454 24 24 24 and in Northern Ireland you can call your local health board (details are in the phone directory or at www.healthandcareni.co.uk); or from a telephone directory, health centre, local pharmacy, hospital, midwife, health visitor or advice centre.

Episode 8

- You can repeat some of the activities that your son or daughter has done at school or college. Activity One, *Sex: yes or no?* (p 65), would be useful to start talking generally about sexual activity, and to explain your family's views about sex. You could add your own 'reasons' to the list to fit with your views.

Sex is not the end of the story. Your relationship with your child is crucial whatever happens. Make it easy for you both to talk – and listen. This will help your son or daughter to be safe, not to get pregnant, and to survive if the relationship ends.

Making time can be difficult, so think about how much time you spend now with your child, and how you could make more if you needed to.

You may be able to identify other important adults for your child to talk to; perhaps an older brother or sister, an uncle or an aunt, or a close family friend.

Sexual choices and sexual health

It seems that some young people are ignoring – or are ignorant of – the messages about safer sex, and cases of HIV and other sexually transmitted infections (STIs) continue to rise. It's clear that more needs to be done to get the message across.

This chapter does not set out to describe the many sexually transmitted infections, their symptoms or treatment. A brief factsheet is provided, but comprehensive resources are available elsewhere, including **fpa**, with detailed information. This material focuses on the risk of transmission through sexual activity and indicates risky behaviour.

It's not easy to explain how sexual infections are transmitted unless students have an understanding of male and female private parts and their function; and we have to make sure of this before we start. The simplest message we can give to people with learning disabilities is always to use a condom in any sexual contact. This can be taught without any reference to contraception if necessary.

The material in this chapter is introduced in stories about some of Tom and Debbie's circle of friends and their sexual behaviour. The stories focus on Brad's risky behaviour and its consequences.

The material in this chapter discusses these areas:

- ⟩ **risky sexual behaviour**
- ⟩ **how STIs are transmitted**
- ⟩ **visiting a sexual health or genitourinary medicine (GUM) clinic**
- ⟩ **using a condom**
- ⟩ **sexual variation.**

Karen talks to Debbie

Karen says, 'I think you are really lucky with Tom. He's so kind and romantic. I really want a boyfriend. Do you think Jake likes me?'

Debbie says 'Well I'm sure he likes you but he won't go out with you.'

'Why not, what's wrong with me?' asks Karen.

'Nothing is wrong with you; it's just that Jake is gay. He doesn't fancy girls. He's with his boyfriend, Ben' says Debbie.

Letter to a magazine

ACTIVITY 1

→ Read the 'Aunty' letter aloud.

→ Read the reply.

→ Ask students whether they think this is good advice.

→ Invite them to think of other advice they might give Karen.

→ Discuss why Karen might want a boyfriend. Does everyone have to be in a relationship?

Dear Aunty,

I need some help. I am at college and I do not have a boyfriend. All my friends have got boyfriends and I feel left out. I try to look good and fashionable, but no one asks me out. I do not know how to talk to boys and I get embarrassed. Why does no one fancy me?

Karen

Dear Karen,

I am sure you look great. Sometimes we all feel that we are the one left out but I'm sure there will be other girls who do not have boyfriends. What is important is feeling good about yourself and doing things that make you feel happy. Develop your own interests and try not to think about boys all the time! Have fun with your female friends, and find new hobbies. If you think you are interesting then I'm sure a boy will think you are too. You will find that you will be less embarrassed talking to boys if you have something to talk about that you enjoy.

Aunty

ACTIVITY 2

About homosexuality

● Jake is gay. This offers an opportunity to discuss aspects of homosexuality, and to be clear that it's OK to be gay. The discussion would usefully include issues around homophobia and bullying. Here are some possible questions to start the discussion.

● Why doesn't Karen realise Jake is gay? Is gayness obvious?

● Are there any problems Jake and his boyfriend might meet because they are gay?

● What difference might it make to their lives?

Episode 2: Brad is a nuisance

In the canteen

2

'How are you two lovely ladies today? Looking very attractive. Can I get you coffee?' says Brad. Debbie pushes off Brad's arm and says 'Oh Brad. Go away will you?' She doesn't like how Brad is standing too close to her and touching her. Karen would like Brad to notice her and so she agrees to let him get her a coffee.

Practise your lines –
avoiding unwanted approaches

● Ask students what other ways Debbie might use to stop Brad.

● Role play the situation, practising students' suggestions and developing the situation.

● Ask students to say how effective each response might be.

Other things you can do

● Practise assertive skills: refer back to *Getting what you want* (p 27).

Episode 3: Brad and Martina

Martina is cross

Martina saw Brad and Karen together in the canteen and she is cross. Brad is supposed to be her boyfriend and he chats up other girls whenever he gets the chance. Martina says 'I don't know if I can trust you – you would go after any woman in the college.' Brad says he was just being friendly and Martina shouldn't nag him. 'Anyway, you're my best girl. How about I come round later and we watch a sexy video together?' Martina agrees.

Can I trust my boyfriend?

This is a sophisticated activity based on quizzes in teenage magazines and may require a good level of understanding or literacy. There are different ways of using it, depending on students' abilities.

Method 1

- Read out the first scene from Activity Sheet 4 (p 94).

- Ask pairs or small groups to decide whether she can trust her boyfriend. What is he doing that makes her think she can't trust him?

- Read the three possible answers one at a time. Ask students whether this is what the young woman would think.

Method 2

- Give each student a copy of the Activity Sheet.

- Read each scene in turn, and the three possible answers.

- Students mark their answer on their own sheet.

- Discuss and compare the answers students have chosen.

Method 3

- Give a copy to each student and ask them to complete it individually or in pairs.

- Discuss and compare the answers students have chosen.

- Students can score themselves if they wish: c = 5, b=2, a =1.

- A higher score means the student is recognising good ways of dealing with issues of trust in a relationship.

Other things you can do

● Change the scenes so it is a young woman who is untrustworthy. Does this affect the suggestions students make?

● Role play the scenes. This can help students understand the different points of view and gives them a chance to practise lines to be clear and assertive in relationships.

Discussion

● **Why does Martina continue to be involved with Brad?**

● **Why does Brad suggest a 'sexy video'?**

The issue of pornography could be raised here. Some students may have access to internet material at home, and potentially easy access to chat rooms.

ACTIVITY SHEET 4: Can I trust my boyfriend?

What would you do?

Tick a) b) or c) to show what you would do in these situations.

1 You are waiting at the cinema and your boyfriend is half an hour late. He makes excuses and claims to have left his phone at home so he couldn't ring you. Later you see it in his pocket.

- ☐ a) You think there must be a good reason for this because he loves you.

- ☐ b) You are worried about it but say nothing. You think he will stop going out with you if you question him.

- ☐ c) You think he is messing you around. You decide to talk to him about what has happened and ask him why he is not telling you the truth.

2 You see your boyfriend talking to two girls at college. He has his arms round them and is being charming and chatty.

- ☐ a) You walk away. You don't mention it when you see him later because if you talk to him, it will make his behaviour worse.

- ☐ b) You join them and put your arm around him drawing him away from the others, making a joke about it.

- ☐ c) You make time to talk to him about it in private and tell him how it makes you feel.

3 Your boyfriend asks to borrow some money from you. You give him £10.00. After two weeks he still has not given it back and makes excuses when you mention it.

- ☐ a) You forget about it because love is not about money.

- ☐ b) You decide that you will make sure you never lend him money again.

- ☐ c) You talk to him about the importance of being able to trust him. You say that he must pay you back when he says he will. Ask him when he plans to do so.

Episode 4: Brad and his girlfriends

Brad and Martina make love

Brad's girlfriend is Martina. They have been going out for three months. Sometimes they have sex. Martina says 'I'm scared of getting a baby.' 'Oh, don't worry' says Brad. 'I'll be careful.'

'What about AIDS?' asks Martina. 'We could use a condom.'

'I hate condoms' says Brad, 'Sex isn't so good with one of those on. If you love me you'll do it with me without a condom.'

'Will you promise to be careful?' asks Martina.

'Of course I will.'

So Martina and Brad make love in the bed. He puts his penis inside her vagina and his sperm goes inside her.

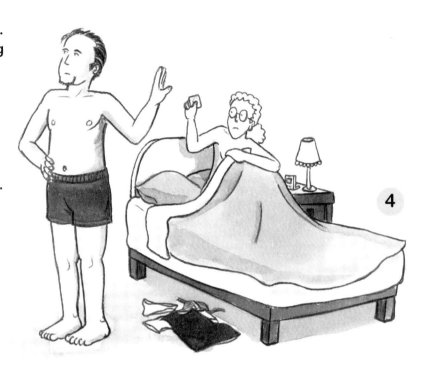

Brad and Cassie

One night Brad went to a party. Martina couldn't go. She had college work to do. At the party Brad saw a girl called Cassie. They smiled at each other. They drank beer and danced really close. They felt very sexy together. After the party Brad went back to Cassie's house and they had sex without a condom.

4

5

What happens?

Read the story and use these questions to explore what students know about catching STIs.

What happens if:

> Cassie has an STI?

> Brad gets an STI from Cassie? Will Martina get it too?

> Brad has sex with someone else? Will they get an STI too?

ACTIVITY 2

Catching a sexually transmitted infection

(This activity can be used to teach specifically about HIV)

- Prepare a range of pictures of a variety of people: male and female, from different backgrounds etc. Magazines are useful for this.

- Choose one of the pictures and announce that this character has an STI. Give the character a name.

- Invite students to choose a partner for the first character.

- Ask students to invent sexual situations for this pair and the other characters (or the teacher could invent them).

- How long does it take for the STI to move round the whole group if they have unprotected sex?

- How does it stop it if they have protected sex?

Other things you can do

If students find this activity difficult, place a mark on the character who has an STI. A condom can be placed between some couples as a concrete example of protection.

Episode 5: Brad goes to the clinic

Brad is worried

Brad is feeling worried. When he goes to the toilet, it feels sore when he pees. Jake asks him to come and play football. 'No' says Brad, 'I don't feel well.'

Jake is sympathetic and Brad decides to trust him and tells him 'It hurts when I pee and there is this yellow stuff coming out of my penis.' Jake says he may have an infection and should go and see a doctor, either his GP or at the clinic.

6

Brad at the clinic

The doctor tells Brad that he understands he may be embarrassed but it is important that he looks at his penis. He has to find out what the infection is and what to do about it so that Brad can get well. He says he will need to do some tests to help him find out what the infection is.

7

What Brad has to do

When Brad is dressed the doctor gives him a prescription to get some tablets from the chemist. He says 'You must always use a condom whenever you have sex. A condom helps stop you getting infections like this and will make sure your girlfriend does not get pregnant. It's a good idea to tell people you have had sex with in case they have the infection too. We can do this for you, and we won't mention your name.'

8

 # Using the factsheet

Talk through factsheet 3 to clarify what students know about sexually transmitted infections. Further material may be needed to increase students' knowledge (see Useful resources).

Activity sheet 3 can be revisited to reaffirm the importance of using a condom in any sexual encounter.

Discussion

 Is there anything that might persuade Brad, Martina and Cassie to stop their risky behaviour?

Further information

ACTIVITY SHEET 3: **Using a male condom** (see p 77)

FACTSHEET 3: **Sexually transmitted infections**

FACTSHEET 3: Sexually transmitted infections

Sexually transmitted infections (STIs) can be spread through vaginal, anal or oral sex with an infected partner and sometimes by sharing sex toys. Both men and women can get and pass on STIs. There are many different STIs – some of the most common are genital warts, genital herpes, chlamydia, gonorrhoea, HIV, trichomonas vaginalis, syphilis and hepatitis B.

Symptoms

Not all STIs have noticeable signs or symptoms, so it's possible to have an infection, and pass it on, without knowing. If there are signs and symptoms, they may include:

- ❯ unusual discharge from the vagina or penis
- ❯ pain or burning when passing urine
- ❯ itches, rashes, lumps or blisters around the genitals or anus
- ❯ pain and/or bleeding during sex
- ❯ pain between periods
- ❯ bleeding after sex
- ❯ pain in the testicles or lower abdomen.

Treatment

Most sexually transmitted infections can be treated and it is usually best if treatment is started as soon as possible. Some infections, such as HIV and genital herpes, never leave the body but there are drugs available that can reduce symptoms and help prevent or delay the development of complications. If left untreated, many sexually transmitted infections can be painful or uncomfortable, and can permanently damage a person's health and fertility, and can be passed on to someone else.

Where to go for help

All tests and treatments are available at a GUM or sexual health clinic. General practices, contraception clinics, young people's services and some pharmacies may also provide testing for some infections. If they can't provide what is needed, they will be able to give details of the nearest service that can.

(continued)

All advice, information and tests are free, but attending a general practice may mean there is a prescription charge for any treatment. Young people under 16, including those with learning disabilities, can be given information, tests and treatment without informing their parents, if they understand what is happening.

◗ Information on all clinics can be obtained from **sexual health direct**, run by **fpa**, on 0845 122 8690 or visit www.fpa.org.uk.

◗ Details of all services, including general practices and pharmacies, can be obtained from www.nhsdirect.nhs.uk. In England and Wales people can call NHS Direct on 0845 46 47, in Scotland NHS 24 on 08454 24 24 24 and in Northern Ireland the local health board (details are in the phone directory or at www.healthandcareni.co.uk).

◗ Details of your nearest contraception, GUM or sexual health clinic can be obtained from a telephone directory, health centre, local pharmacy, hospital, midwife, health visitor or advice centre.

◗ Details of GUM or sexual health clinics are available from the Sexual Health Information Line on 0800 567 123 or at www.playingsafely.co.uk. Details of young people's services can be obtained from Brook on 0800 0185 023 or from Sexwise on 0800 28 29 30, or at www.ruthinking.co.uk.

Partner notification

When someone has an STI it is very important that their current sexual partner(s) and any other recent partners are also tested and treated. The staff at the clinic or general practice can discuss with service users which of their sexual partners may need to be tested.

Service users may be given a 'contact slip' to send to or give to their partner(s) or, with permission, the clinic can do this for them. The slip explains that the partner(s) may have been exposed to an STI and suggests that they go for a check-up. It may or may not say what the infection is. It will not have on it the name of the person who has the infection, so confidentiality is protected. It is recommended that people tell their partner(s), but it isn't compulsory.

Further information

fpa offers information and advice on STIs and has a wide range of leaflets.
(See useful contacts p 119)

Episode 6: Steve is HIV positive

Tom at the clinic with Steve

9

Tom has just heard that his friend Steve has got the infection HIV which cannot be cured. All Steve's friends are upset. Tom tries to reassure him that the sexual health clinic or hospital will have good medicines to help him. Steve is really cross with himself because he did not use a condom when he had sex, and caught the infection.

 # Can you get rid of the HIV virus?

This activity demonstrates that the HIV virus spreads through body systems and that once in the body it cannot be removed.

 You will need:

— A jar with red coloured water to represent blood.
— A small amount of blue dye to represent the HIV virus.

How to do it:

Explain that the HIV virus can pass from one person to another when they have sex without a condom. It then gets into the person's blood system.

Show students the jar with red liquid and say that it represents blood.

Explain that the blue dye represents the HIV virus.

Place a small amount of the blue dye in the red liquid. Ask the students what has happened. The liquid is now purple.

Ask students if the liquid can be changed back to its original red colour.

Explain that in the same way the HIV virus cannot be removed from the bloodstream once it has entered it.

[This activity is adapted from *Let's Do It*, Image in Action 1997]

- ⮞ Both sexes are liable to catch HIV from unprotected sex.

- ⮞ The infection rate for heterosexuals is rising. Why might this be?

- ⮞ Opportunity to explain about HIV infection and treatment (see info below).

- ⮞ Stress the importance of using a condom in all sexual encounters.

Further information

FACTSHEET 3:   Sexually transmitted infections

Supporting work to do at home

- ⮞ Find out where your nearest sexual health clinic is. Does it have sessions for young people? You can get details from your phone book, health centre or hospital or from **fpa**.

- ⮞ Let your son or daughter know that s/he can always talk to you. Try to keep the lines of communication open even if it seems difficult sometimes. You may be able to help them sort out a problem before it becomes a crisis!

What does the future hold?

This chapter looks briefly at some of the possible future relationships of the characters in the stories. Not every relationship ends in long term partnership, and we must try to avoid denying people with learning disabilities the same range and choices in relationships that other people have. Debbie and Tom may find several other partners; Brad may settle down happily with Martina – we can never know.

Other stories can be added, with other scenarios. We have included a story about Asima in the future, to provide an opportunity to discuss customs in different cultures.

This material provides opportunities to discuss students' hopes and assumptions about their future relationships; and to consider realistic options. Life isn't all a bowl of cherries for any of us; and the options available to people with learning disabilities can be more restricted than for others. But we should make sure that we don't close options that are possible, even if they require harder work.

Tom and Debbie: Scenario 1

Tom and Debbie split up

Tom and Debbie were boyfriend and girlfriend for about six months, then they started to find that they didn't have anything to talk about any more. Their habits began to annoy each other and they stopped fancying each other. They decided to break up and have time to themselves. After a couple of months, Tom met Mandy and they became boyfriend and girlfriend. Debbie is having a good time with her friends and working hard at her studying. She doesn't want a boyfriend at the moment.

Tom and Debbie: Scenario 2

Their own flat

Tom and Debbie were boyfriend and girlfriend for a year. They were spending all their time travelling between each other's houses. They decided they would like to move in together. They found a flat they both liked that was convenient for town and not too far from their families. They had to learn a lot about cleaning, cooking and going to the launderette but they shared all the jobs.

Debbie joined Tom and his family on their summer holiday at the seaside. Tom went with Debbie on her first day when she started working in the supermarket. Debbie's mother bought them a fantastic portable CD player for Christmas.

Of course they quarrelled sometimes. Debbie wanted to play tennis with her friends rather than go out with Tom. Tom spent ages on his latest computer game rather than be with Debbie, but they found ways to sort out their differences and their relationship got stronger as they worked through their arguments.

They still find it great fun being together.

Tom and Debbie: Scenario 3

Tom and Debbie get married

Tom and Debbie were together for four years. They both got jobs and shared a flat. They were really in love and decided to get married. Maybe they would start a family soon. They bought a flat together rather than rented one.

[This can be a chance to discuss weddings and marriages from different faiths and cultures. Show pictures of a range of wedding ceremonies and situations (eg registry office, place of worship) and the different clothes and colours that are associated with marriage. Explain what promises are made and discuss with the group how they are similar and different in range of cultures and faiths.]

Tom and Debbie: Scenario 4

The new baby

After six years of being together Tom and Debbie decided that they wanted to start a family. They stopped using contraception when they had sex and after a few months, Debbie became pregnant. When she had a baby girl, everyone was delighted. But Debbie and Tom had not realised how much hard work a new baby can mean. They were really pleased that their families were there to help them.

Discussion

⮕ Do all relationships become permanent?

⮕ How can people cope when a relationship comes to an end?

⮕ Why might a couple like Tom and Debbie want to get married?

⮕ What are the realities of bringing up children? What support might be needed to help people with learning disabilities manage? How might the rights and needs of a child be balanced against the desires and needs of parents?

Brad and Martina

Martina is pregnant

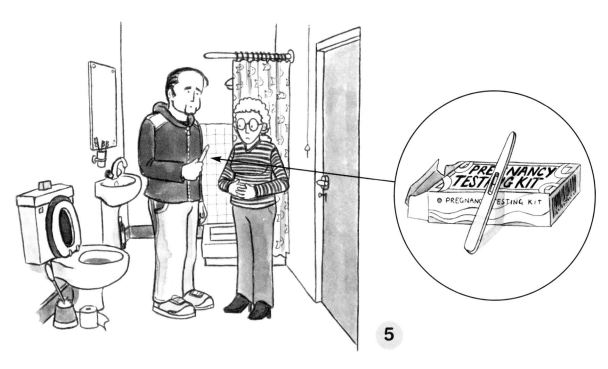

5

Brad and Martina did not use a condom when they had sex and Martina became pregnant. Neither of them wanted the baby but they did not know what to do or where to go for help.

Discussion

What could they do?

— They could decide that Martina carries on being pregnant and then has the baby.

— They could decide that the baby, once born, could be given up for adoption.

— They could have used emergency contraception when they knew they had had unsafe sex.

— They could seek advice about Martina having an abortion and ending the pregnancy.

Further information

FACTSHEET 4: Options for unplanned pregnancy

Making a decision

The decision about whether to continue with an unplanned pregnancy and keep the baby, have the baby adopted, or have an abortion is not an easy one to make. When a woman has a learning disability this can add further complexities.

A woman with a learning disability may find it helpful to talk to her partner, friends and family or the doctor or nurse at her general practice. Other professionals may also become involved, for example, in the case of a young woman, her head teacher, her social worker, an educational psychologist and a school nurse. An adult may seek support from the community learning disability team, community nurses or her care worker. Support may include staff assessing her understanding of her situation and of the information given to her and her ability to consent to and understand the consequences of following the different options.

There are several organisations which provide counselling but ensure that they understand how to counsel a woman with a learning disability who may choose to have an advocate accompany her. There are some organisations that offer pregnancy testing and counselling but believe that abortion is morally wrong. They will not provide balanced information about the options and will counsel against abortion.

The options

This factsheet does not intend to provide precise details associated with each option. Local specialist advice needs to be sought. It does provide a summary of the law around abortion.

⊗ Keeping the baby

This will need family involvement and support; and may involve social services in supporting the well being of the child. Contact the local teenage pregnancy co-ordinator for post birth educational opportunities.

⊗ Adoption

This must be carried out through an adoption agency or social services.

⊗ Abortion

Abortion is legal in Britain under the Abortion Act 1967 as amended by the Human Fertilisation and Embryology Act 1990. The Act says that two doctors must agree that the continuance of the pregnancy would involve risk, greater than if the pregnancy was terminated, of injury to the physical or mental health of the pregnant woman or any existing children of her family.

(continued)

Abortion is legal in the UK regardless of the pregnant woman's age. How easy it is to arrange and abortion can vary throughout the UK, and it can be more difficult to obtain an abortion in Northern Ireland. Abortion is safer and easier the earlier it is done in pregnancy.

Abortion and under 16s

A woman under 16 can have an abortion without telling her parents. The doctors will encourage her to involve her parents or another supportive adult, but if she chooses not, she can still have an abortion if both doctors believe that she fully understands what is involved and it is in her best interests.

Women with learning disabilities

The terms of the Abortion Act apply to women with learning disabilities and a woman could have an abortion, providing the criteria of the Act are fulfilled and she is able to understand the procedure. No operation may be performed on a woman without her consent (see Factsheet 1, page 68, for more information about capacity to consent). If a woman is not competent to make this decision for herself, then a declaration must be sought. This is a legal process outlined in the Mental Capacity Act 2005.

What does an abortion involve?

Abortion is a safe and effective procedure. Abortion is not entirely risk-free, but it is safer than going through pregnancy and having a baby. There are different abortion procedures and the method used depends on how long the woman has been pregnant. An abortion service should ideally be able to offer a choice of abortion methods. All women should have good information and counselling and be advised of any complications or side effects that may occur.

Further information
....

fpa offers information and advice on abortion and a leaflet *Abortion – your questions answered* is available.

Living with HIV

6

Steve often meets his friends on a trip to their favourite country pub. They are all anxious about Steve who has HIV. But Steve tells them he is keeping well and enjoying his job at the garage. He has not developed AIDS because he takes the medicines from the doctor.

Discussion

> Drugs are available so that people infected with HIV can remain fit and able to lead their normal lives.

> There is still prejudice about HIV and AIDS and young people in particular may face problems if they reveal their HIV status.

At the birthday party

Asima's family would like her to get married. When they go to family parties like her cousin's birthday, she is introduced to young men her mother hopes she will like. Asima is interested in these boys and she plans to make up her own mind when she falls in love. She is also keen on studying and plans to do more maths courses in the future.

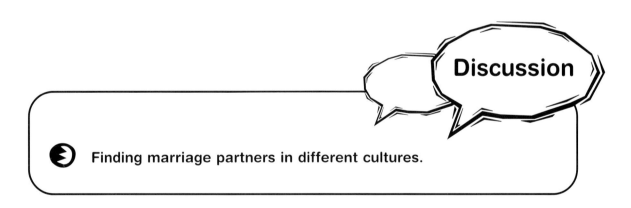

Discussion

> Finding marriage partners in different cultures.

Supporting work to do at home

Discuss with your son/daughter what these various relationships mean. Show them photos of people you know and what happened to them as their relationships unfolded. Try to include different options. You may want to use pictures from magazines or soap opera storylines or stories about celebrities to illustrate other relationship choices, eg divorced couples, gay and lesbian relationships, how people get together (and if they marry) in other cultures.

Useful resources

This list only includes resources which are currently in print and available for purchase. There are however many good resources, which are now out of print. Copies may be available from libraries, or from health promotion units. Some are available from the website **www.me-and-us.com**

A guide to health related resources for people with learning disabilities is available from the Health Development Agency website **www.hda-online.org.uk**. Published in 1999, the guide contains some resources which are now out of print, but provides useful advice on using resources.

Publishers details are listed by the resource, unless they appear in the useful contacts list on p 119.

Resources for young people with learning disabilities

Books beyond words

Royal College of Psychiatrists.
Tel: 020 7235 2351.
www.rcpsych.ac.uk.

A series of illustrated booklets with no words (or very few) designed to assist people with learning disabilities. Subject areas covered include health, emotions and abuse and lifestyle.

Everything you ever wanted to know about safer sex ... but nobody bothered to tell you

Nigel Bull with Camden People First.
Tel: 020 7820 6655.

Information about safer sex and the prevention of HIV for people with learning disabilities.

Jason's private world

Life Support Productions.
Tel: 020 7723 7520.
www.lifesupportproductions.co.uk.

VHS video for men with learning disabilities. Covers consent and saying no, safer sex and condoms.

Kylie's private world

Life Support Productions.

VHS video for women with learning disabilities. Covers periods, sanitary protection, consent and saying no and safer sex.

You, your body and sex

Life Support Productions.

Animated sex and relationships education video for people with learning disabilities.

You, your body and sex DVD

Life Support Productions.

Highlights from Life Support Productions video titles (see above).

Your private parts

Women's Health.
Supplied by The Elfrida Society.
Tel: 020 7359 7443.
www.elfrida.com

Clear information for people with learning disabilities.

Your rights about sex

British Institute of Learning Disabilities.

Sets out in clear language the dos and don'ts around sexual behaviour.

Resources for people who work with young people with learning disabilities

fpa leaflets

A wide range of sexual health leaflets covering contraception, sexually transmitted infections and abortion. Regularly revised and updated. A mail-order catalogue is available from **fpa** 0845 122 8600, or order online at www.fpa.org.uk.

Contraceptive display kit

fpa.

An ideal resource to use with young people when discussing contraception. The kit contains samples of contraceptives, a condom demonstrator, **fpa** leaflets on contraception and a manual containing a variety of exercises. (The exercises are not written for work with young people with learning disabilities.)

Learning disabilities, sex and the law

Claire Fanstone and Sarah Andrews. **fpa**.

Looks at legislation around sexual activity and people with learning disabilities, covering subjects such as capacity to consent, intimate care, record keeping and contraception. Guides staff to seek advice from appropriate people and places.

Sexuality and learning disability: a resource for staff

Claire Fanstone and Zarine Katrak. **fpa**.

Includes a range of creative approaches to working with people with learning disabilities, based on **fpa**'s successful learning disability training courses.

Talking together ... about growing up: a workbook for parents of children with learning disabilities

Lorna Scott and Lesley Kerr-Edwards. **fpa**.

Essential resource to support parents in helping their children, who are approaching or around the age of puberty, understand about growing up. The book covers the life cycle, body parts, public and private, keeping safe, feelings, growing up and looking ahead. It can also be used within the school setting or by schools working in partnership with parents.

Talking together ... about contraception

Lesley Kerr-Edwards and Lorna Scott.
fpa.

A two-book pack to support young people with learning disabilities who wish to access contraception. Book One is a resource for everyone who works with or supports a young person with a learning disability, and should be used in conjunction with Book Two, which has been written for young people with learning disabilities. Includes clear pictures, easy-to-read stories and picture posters.

Body boards and other packs

Headon Ltd. Tel: 0161 998 8877.
www.headonltd.co.uk.

Various visual packs and practical resources.

Chance to choose

Hilary Dixon. Me-and-us Ltd.
Tel: 01539 622 310. www.me-and-us.co.uk.

CD of SRE activities and programmes on various themes.

Confidentiality in schools

Sheila White. Brook.

For teachers, school nurses, school governors and other professionals working with young people. Discusses confidentiality in the context of PSHE and provides ideas for workshop activities.

Faith, values and sex and relationships education

Simon Blake and Zarine Katrak.
NCB Publications.

Book offering curriculum ideas and positive strategies for sex and relationships education in a multi-faith society.

Faith, values and sex and relationships education
Forum factsheet 29

NCB Publications. Tel: 020 7843 6000.
www.ncb.org.uk.

Factsheet looking at the issues involved in developing an approach to SRE which is inclusive of diverse faith perspectives.

Growing and learning about sexual health

Jane Keeling. Tel: 01246 207633.
www.growingandlearning.co.uk.

Parent and carer's toolkits with activities and cards. There are three packs available: working with young women, young men, and about sexual health.

Holding on, letting go. Sex, sexuality and people with learning disabilities

John Drury, Lynne Hutchinson and Jon Wright.
Souvenir Press. Tel: 01235 400400.

Book for parents and carers of people with a learning disability to help them feel more confident when thinking about sexuality in relation to their son or daughter.

Janet's got her period

Boulton Hawker Films Ltd.
Tel: 01449 616200.

Australian video and resource pack intended to help young women with learning disabilities cope with menstruation.

Let's do it: Creative activities for sex education for young people with learning disabilities

R Johns, L Scott and J Bliss.
Image in Action.

Activities using visual images and drama for use in schools, colleges and day centres.

Let's plan it

Lorna Scott and Sarah Duigan.
Image in Action.

A guide to planning programmes of SRE for a wide range of young people with learning disabilities.

Living your life

Ann Craft, re-edited by Sarah Bustard.
Brook.

SRE programme for young people with learning disabilities with worksheets and activities.

Male and female cloth models

Body Sense. Tel: 01684 594 715.
www.bodysense.org.uk.

Anatomically correct, half life-size clothed models, with detailed notes.

Picture Yourself 2: social and sex education for people with learning disabilities

Hilary Dixon. Me-and-us Ltd.

Containing 193 picture cards with educators' notes on CD. Themes include Me as an Individual; Relationships with others; Menstruation and wet dreams; sexual health; Pregnancy, birth and parenthood; single sex relationships.

Protect yourself!

Brook.

Eight teaching programmes on contraception and sexual health (for mainstream pupils but useful information).

Sex and relationships education – a step-by-step guide for teachers

Simon Blake. Fulton Publications.
Tel: 0870 787 1722.
www.fultonpublishers.co.uk.

Includes a chapter on working with young people with learning disabilities.

Sex and relationships education for children and young people with learning difficulties

NCB.

Factsheet looking at defining, planning and delivering SRE, including help on developing a policy.

Sex and the three Rs – rights, responsibilities and risks

Michelle McCarthy and David Thompson.
Pavilion Publications. Tel: 01273 623222.
www.pavpub.com.

A sex and relationships education package for working with adults with learning disabilities.

Talking about homosexuality in the secondary school

Simon Forrest, Grant Biddle, Stephen Clift.
Avert. www.avert.org.

Includes steps schools need to take before discussing the issues and strategies for talking about homosexuality with governors, parents, staff and students.

Teenagers and sexuality

John Coleman. Hodder and Stoughton.
Tel: 01273 693311. www.tsa.uk.com.

Guide for parents wishing to discuss sexuality with their teenagers.

APPENDIX

Useful contacts

fpa

fpa is the UK's leading sexual health charity –
our purpose is to enable people in the UK to
make informed choices about sex and to
enjoy sexual health.

Membership

Become a member of **fpa** and receive a range
of benefits while supporting our vital work.
The benefits include:

- a full set of **fpa** factsheets and leaflets

- quarterly mailings, which include
  subscriptions to *Sex Talk* and *In Brief*

- discounts on **fpa** open training courses

- discounts on **fpa** publications (school and
  organisation members).

Training

fpa provides high quality training in sexual
health, sex and relationships, and sexuality.
We offer:

- Open training: offered on pre-set dates
  and open to all.

- On request training: the same content and
  format as open training but delivered to a
  specific group or organisation.

- Tailor made training: specifically designed
  to meet a client's particular needs, and
  may offer a mix of training and
  consultation.

- Consultancy: **fpa** has a strong team of
  experts in all aspects of sexual health who
  are available to facilitate seminars or
  briefings, to provide specific advice and to
  assist with writing a relevant policy or
  guidelines.

fpa provides accreditation for most of its
courses.

fpa publications

fpa offers a complete mail order service for
health and education professionals and the
public. Our extensive stock includes books,
leaflets and resources on sex and relationships
education, learning disabilities, contraception,
and sexual health.

For more details on membership, training or
publications, or to order publications, see
www.fpa.org.uk or call 020 7608 5240.

Helpline

sexual health direct is a nationwide service
run by **fpa**. It provides:

- confidential information and advice and a
  wide range of leaflets on individual methods
  of contraception, common sexually
  transmitted infections, pregnancy choices,
  abortion and planning a pregnancy

- details of contraception clinics, sexual
  health clinics and genitourinary medicine
  (GUM) clinics.

fpa helplines

England and Wales
helpline 0845 122 8690
9am to 6pm Monday to Friday

Northern Ireland
helpline 028 90 325 488
9am to 5pm Monday to Thursday
9am to 4.30pm Friday

or visit **fpa**'s website **www.fpa.org.uk**

British Institute of Learning Disabilities

Campion House
Green Street
Kidderminster
Worcestershire DY10 1JL
Tel: 01562 723010
www.bild.org.uk

Information, publications, training and consultancy services.

Brook

421 Highgate Studios
53–79 Highgate Road
London NW5 1TL
Tel: 020 7284 6040
www.brook.org.uk

Runs local young people's sexual health services. Produces a range of sexual health resources for young people and those who work with them.

Contact a Family

209–211 City Road
London EC1V 1JN
Helpline: 0808 808 3555
Textphone: 0808 808 3556
www.cafamily.org.uk

Provides support and advice to families with disabled children.

Enable

6th Floor
7 Buchanan Street
Glasgow G1 3HL
Tel: 0141 226 4541
www.enable.org.uk

Membership organisation for people with learning disabilities and their family carers in Scotland.

Image in Action

Chinnor Road
Bledlow Ridge
High Wycombe
Bucks HP14 4AJ
Tel: 01494 481632

Works in schools, colleges and centres, publishes resources and provides training and a consultancy service for organisations providing sex and relationships education for people with learning disabilities.

Mencap

123 Golden Lane
London EC1Y 0RT
Tel: 020 7454 0454
www.mencap.org.uk

Works with people with a learning disability, their families and carers. Has a network of affiliated groups throughout England, Northern Ireland and Wales.

People First

Various regional groups in UK.
www.peoplefirst.org.uk

Organisation run by and for people with learning disabilities. Produces a newsletter and resources.

Sex Education Forum

National Children's Bureau
8 Wakley Street
London EC1V 7QE
Tel: 020 7843 1901
www.ncb.org.uk

Advice and publications on developing sex and relationship policies, working with parents and carers and good practice in delivering sex and relationships education.